LAURIE SIMMONS

Photographs 1978/79

text by **COLLIER SCHORR**

Skarstedt Fine Art, New York

LAURIE SIMMONS

Photographs 1978/79

Interiors and The Big Figures

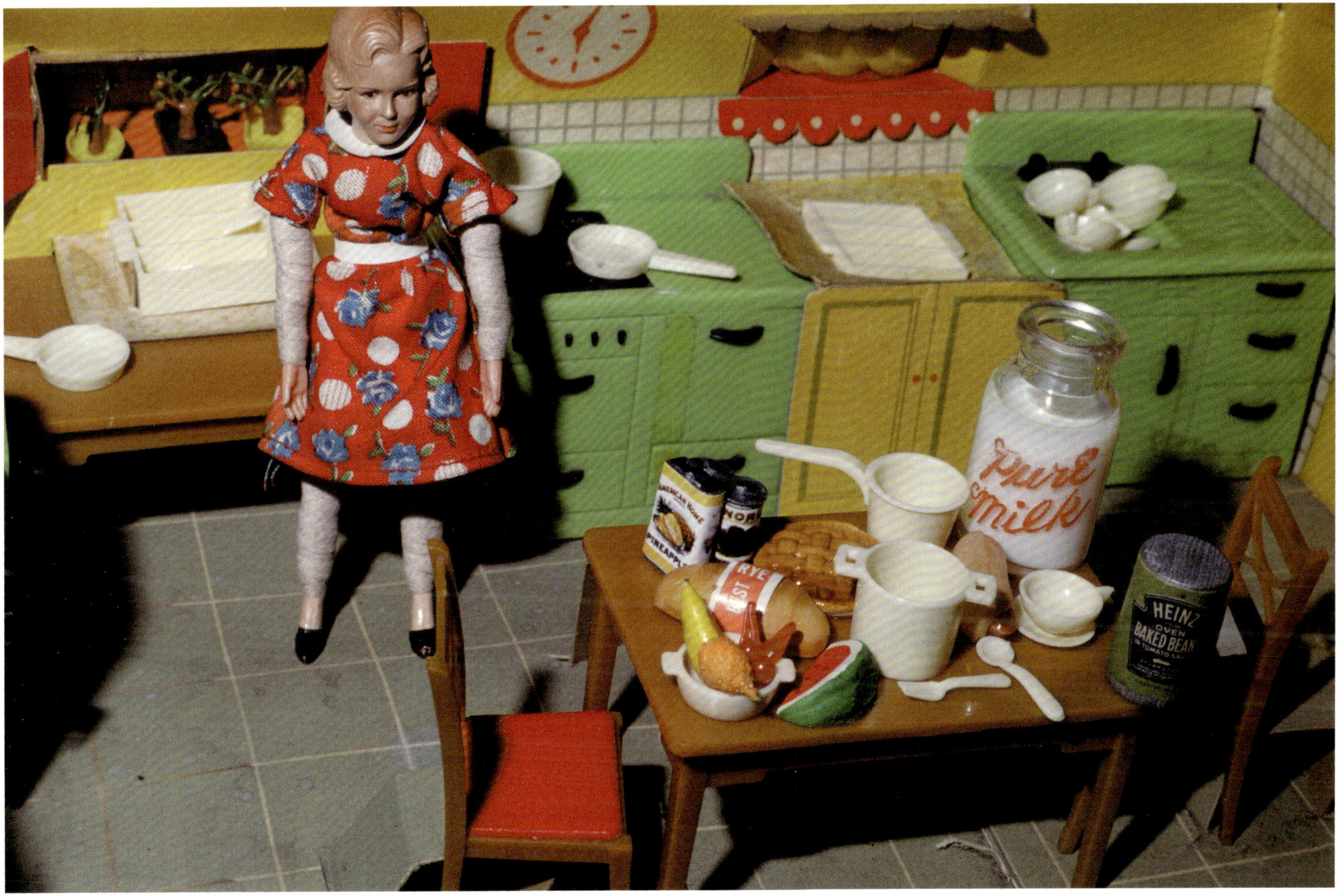
Pure milk
HEINZ
OVEN
RYE

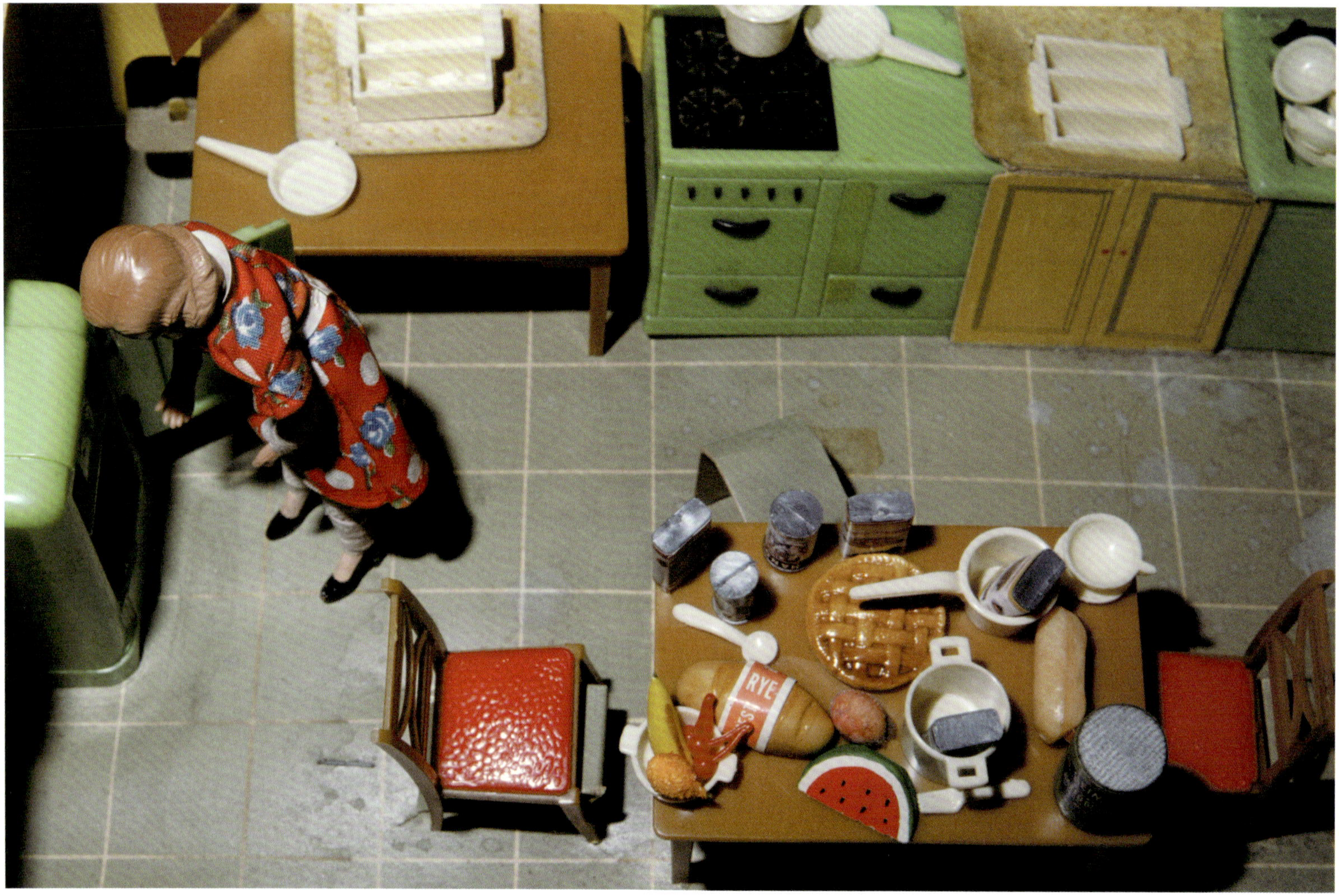
RYE

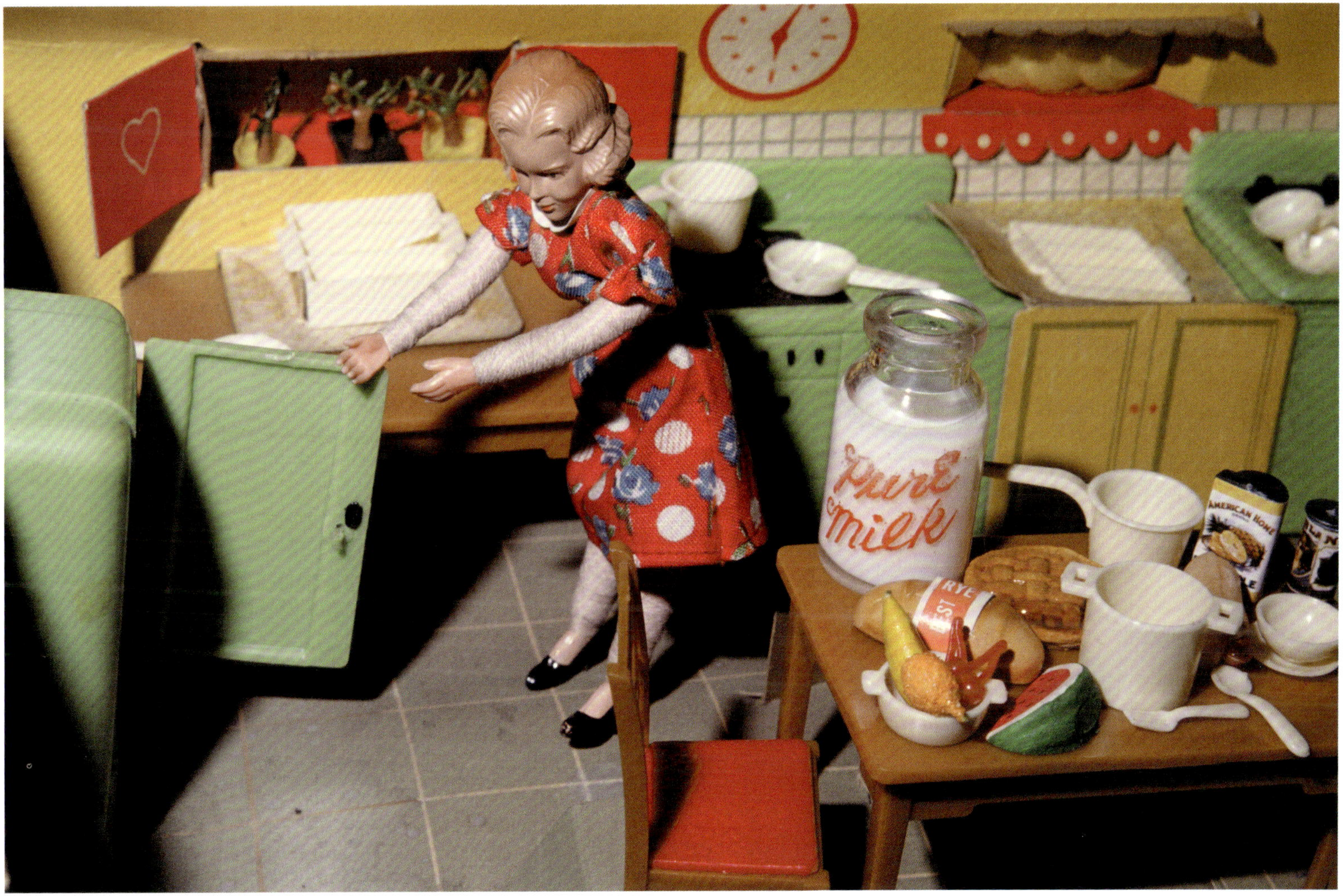
Pure milk
AMERICAN HOME
RYE

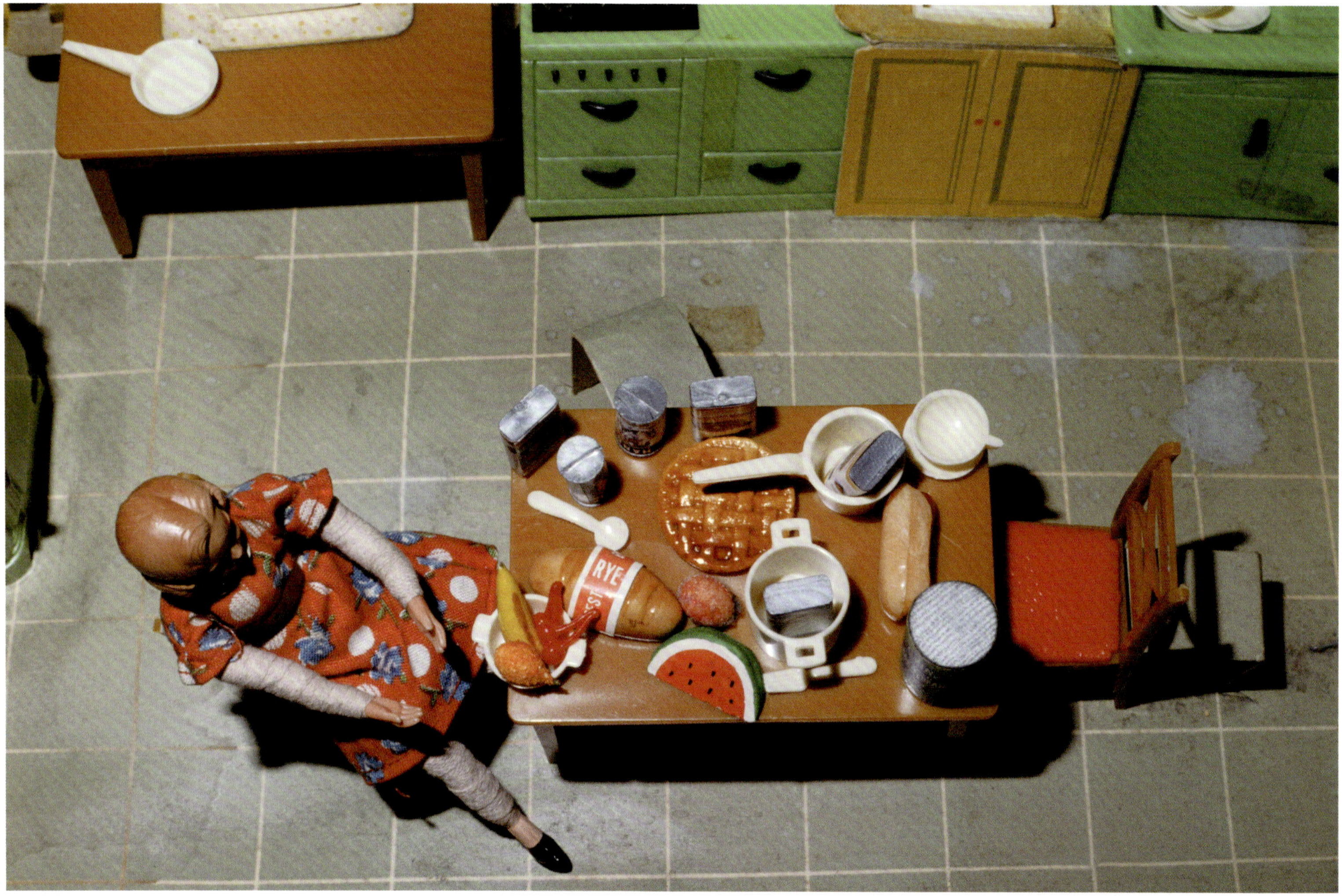
RYE

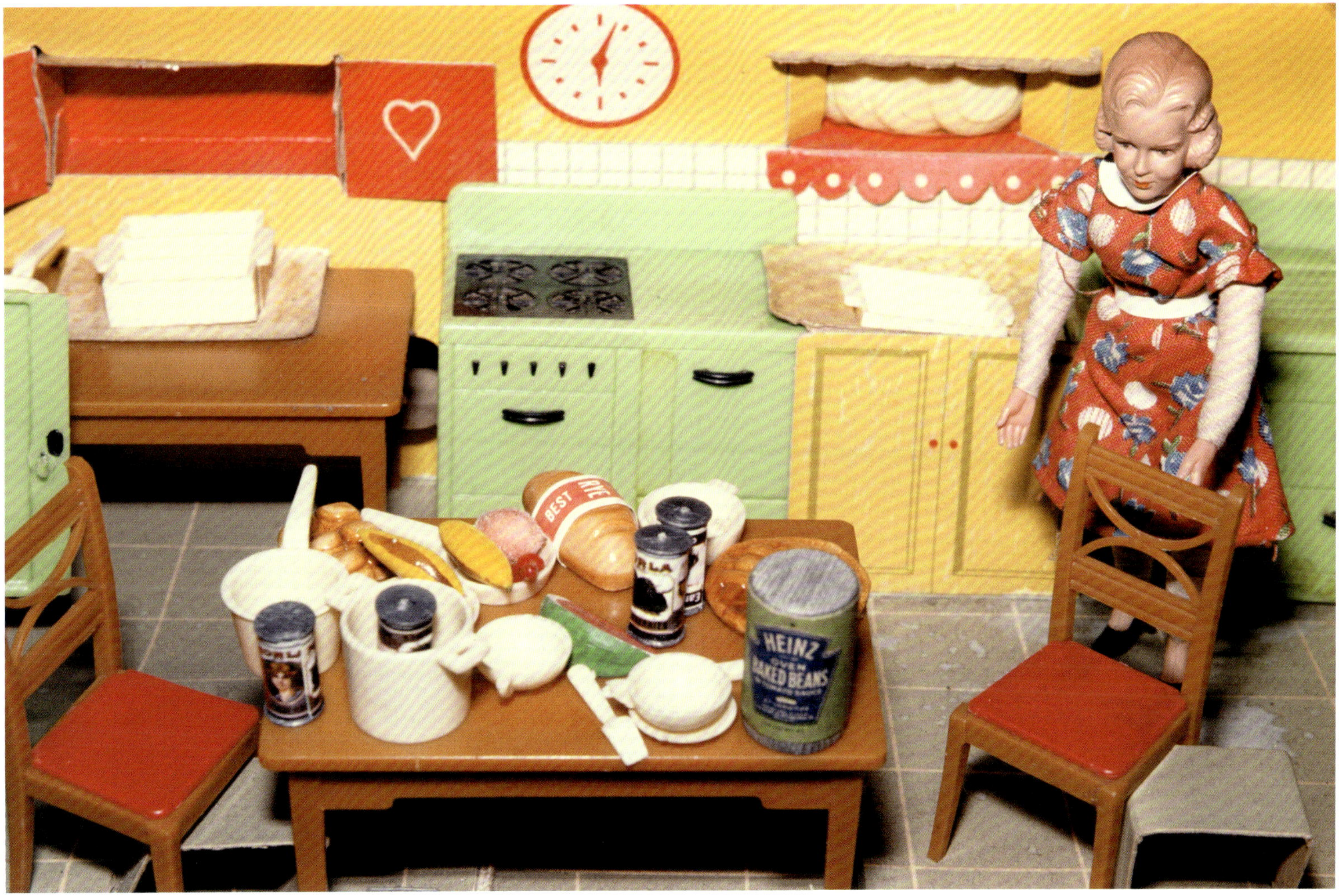
BEST RYE
HEINZ
OVEN
BAKED BEANS

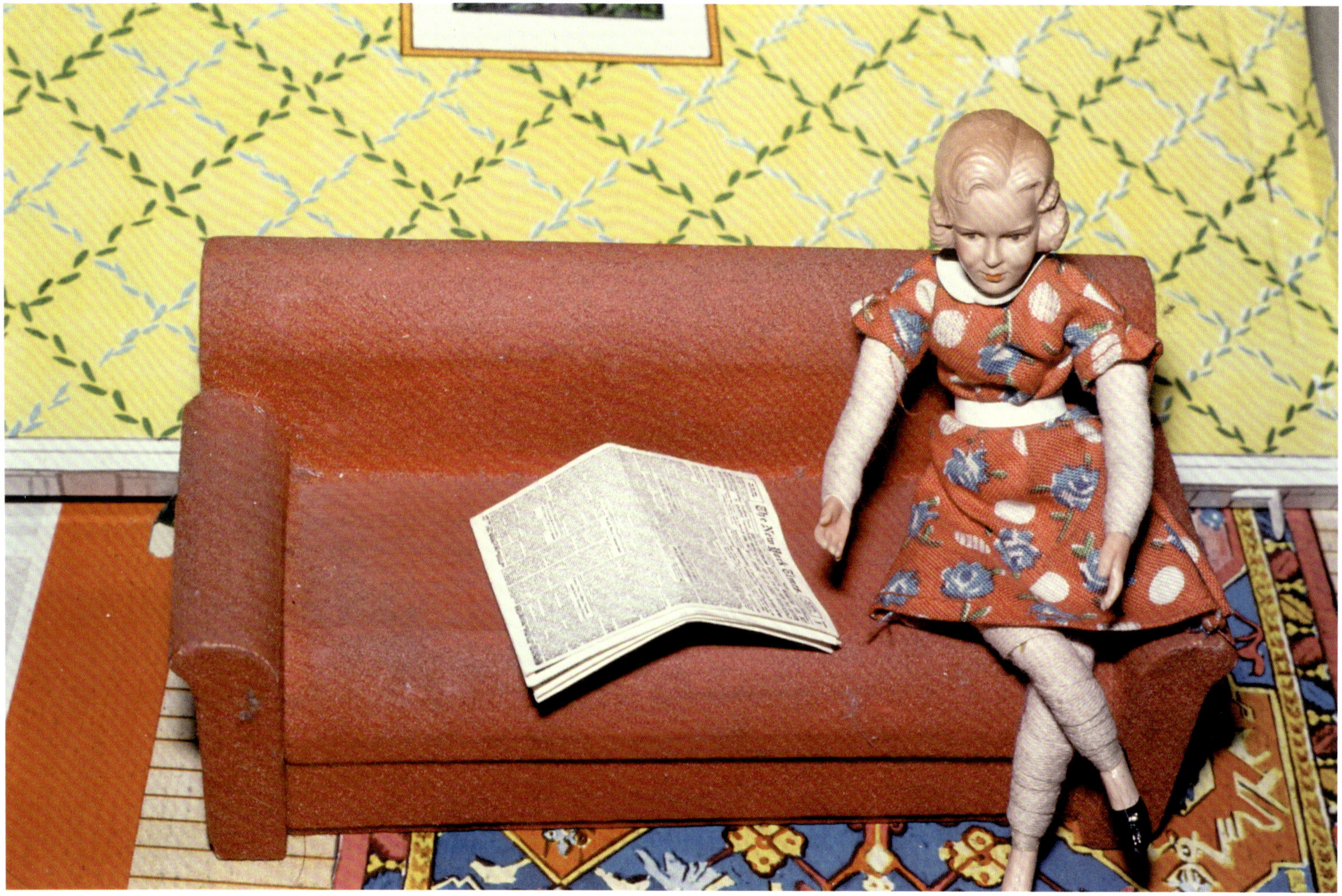
The New York Times

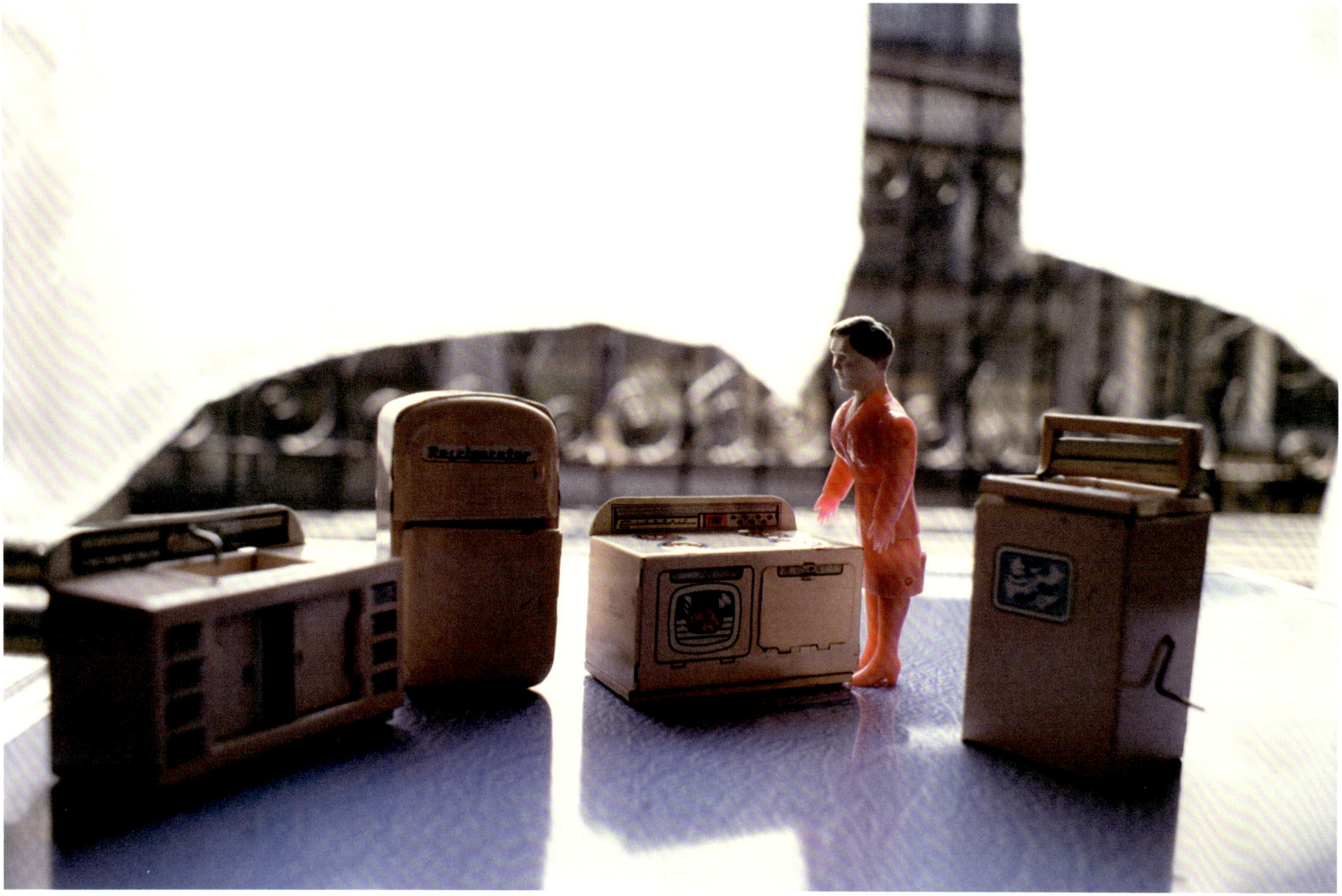

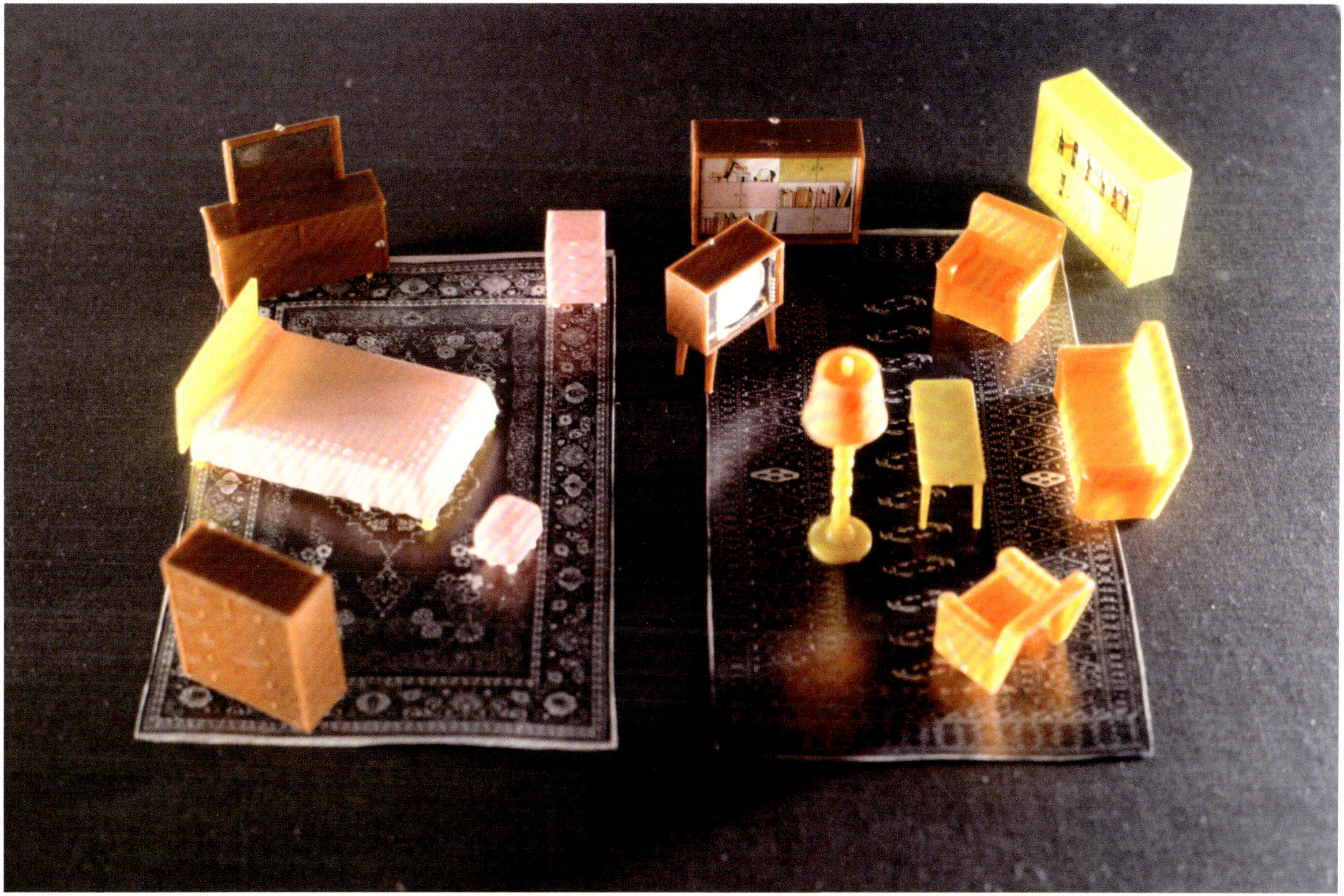

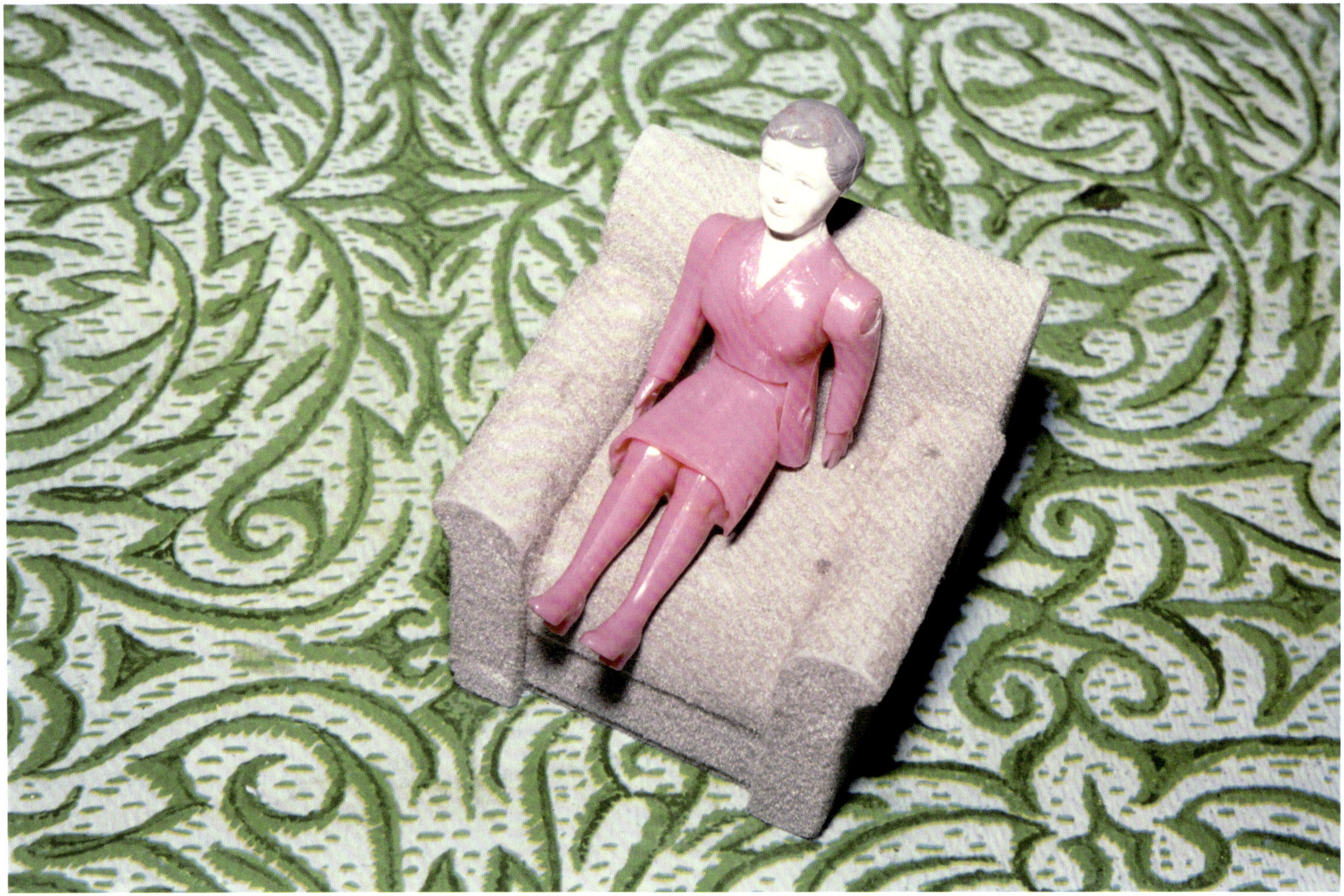

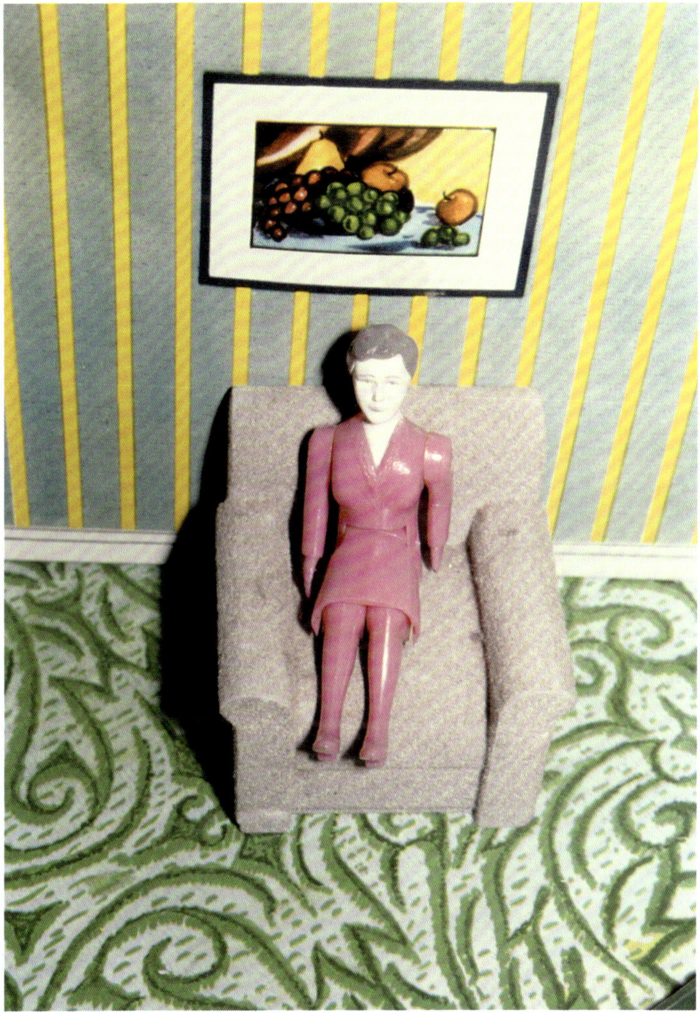

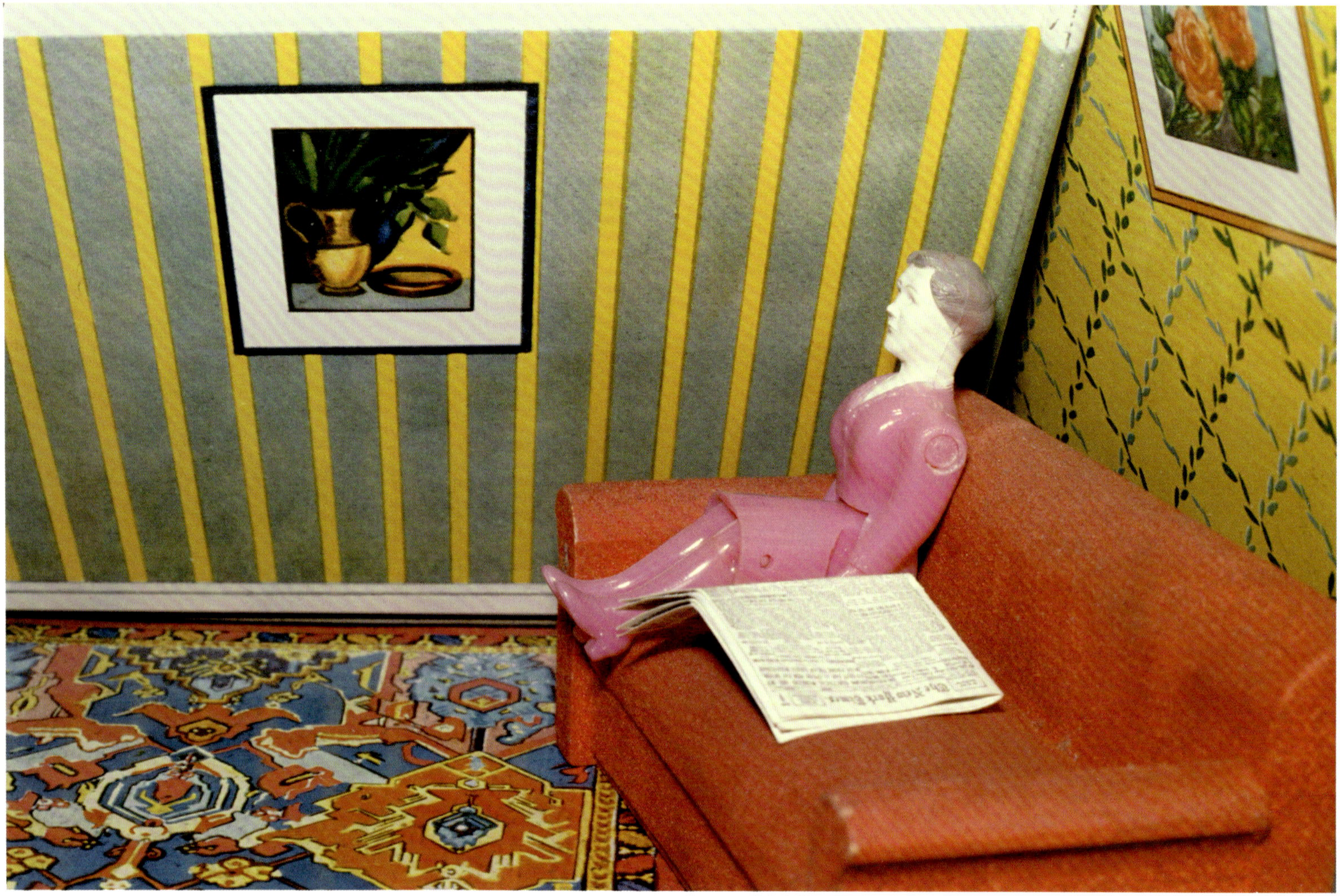

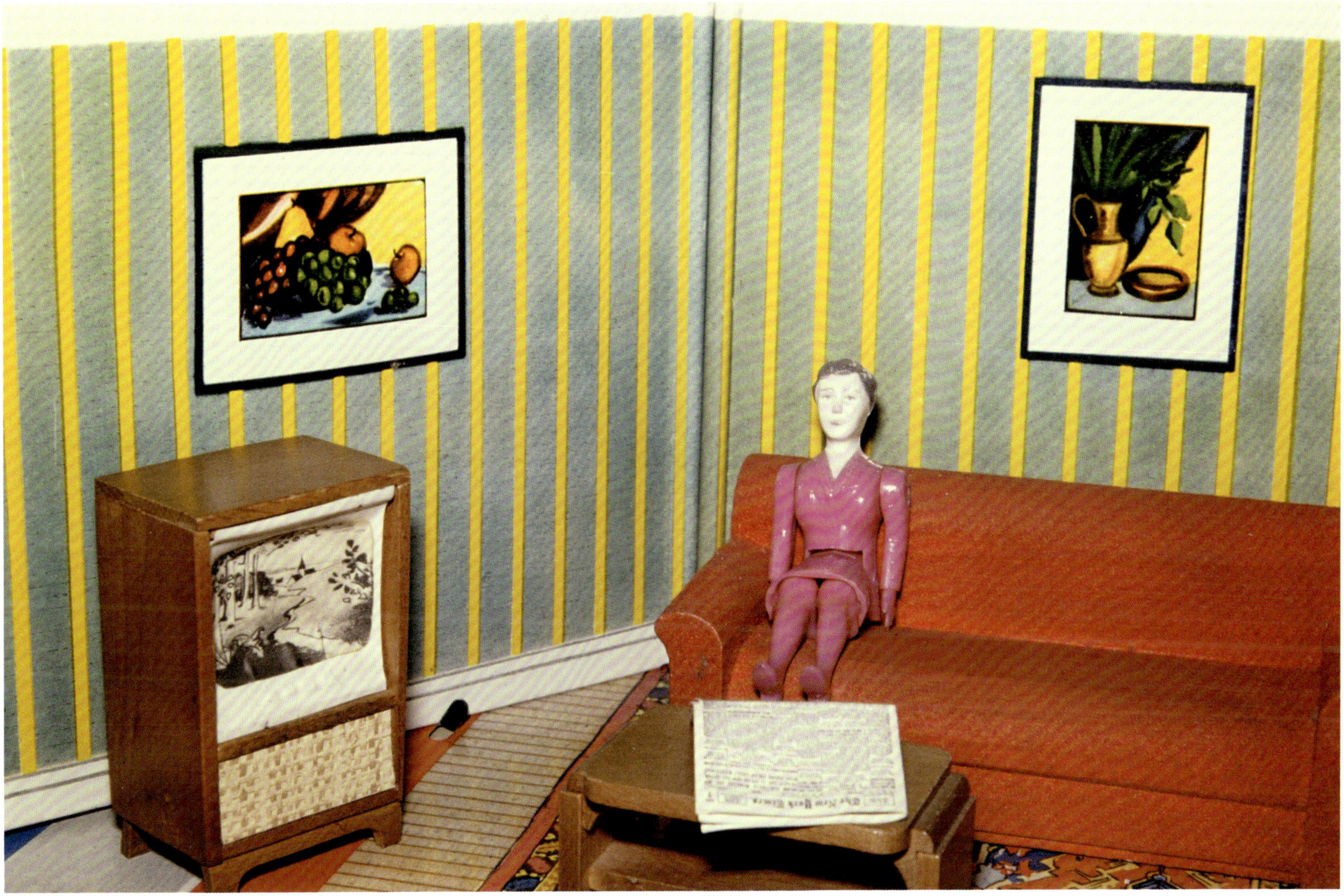

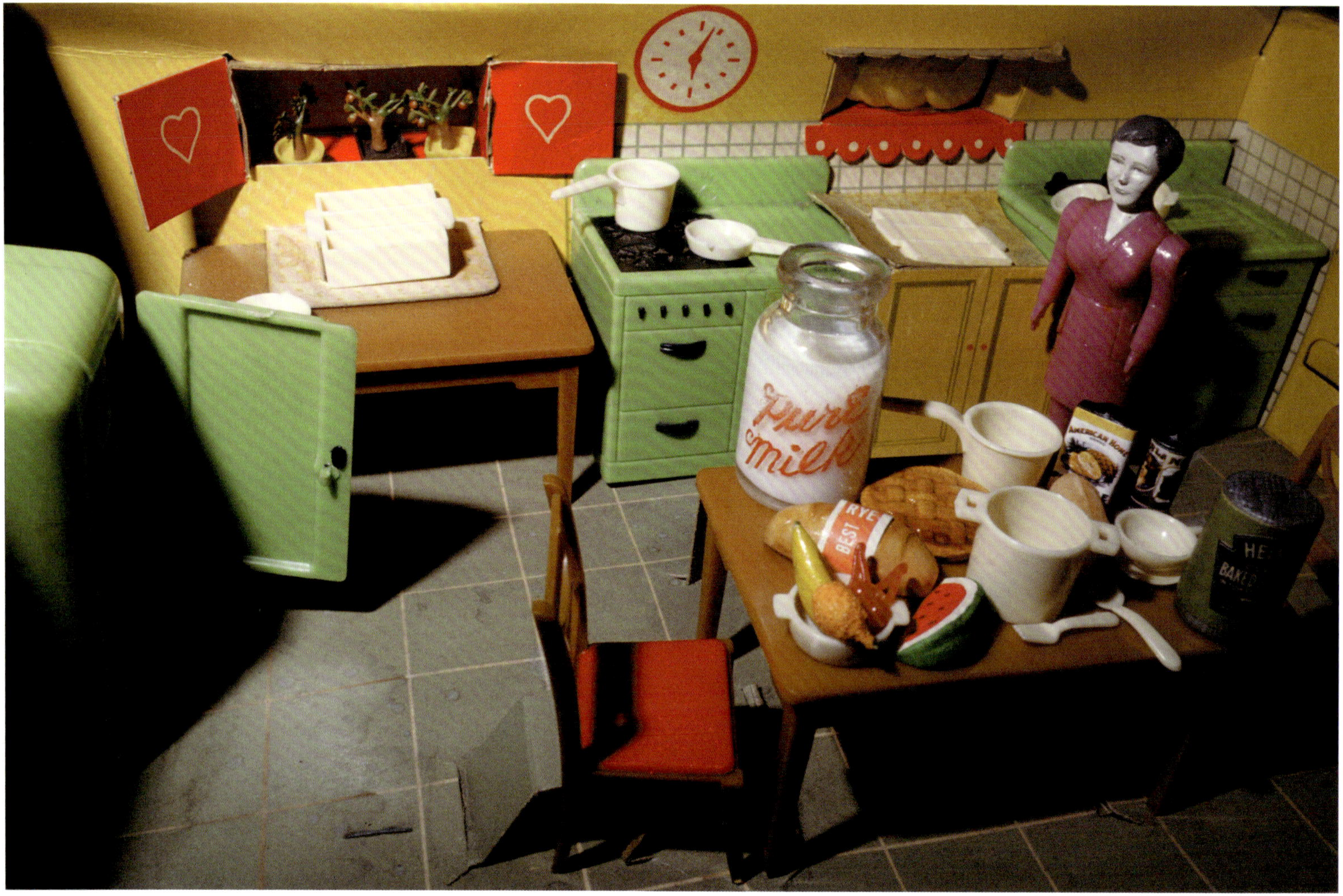
Pure milk
RYE
BEST

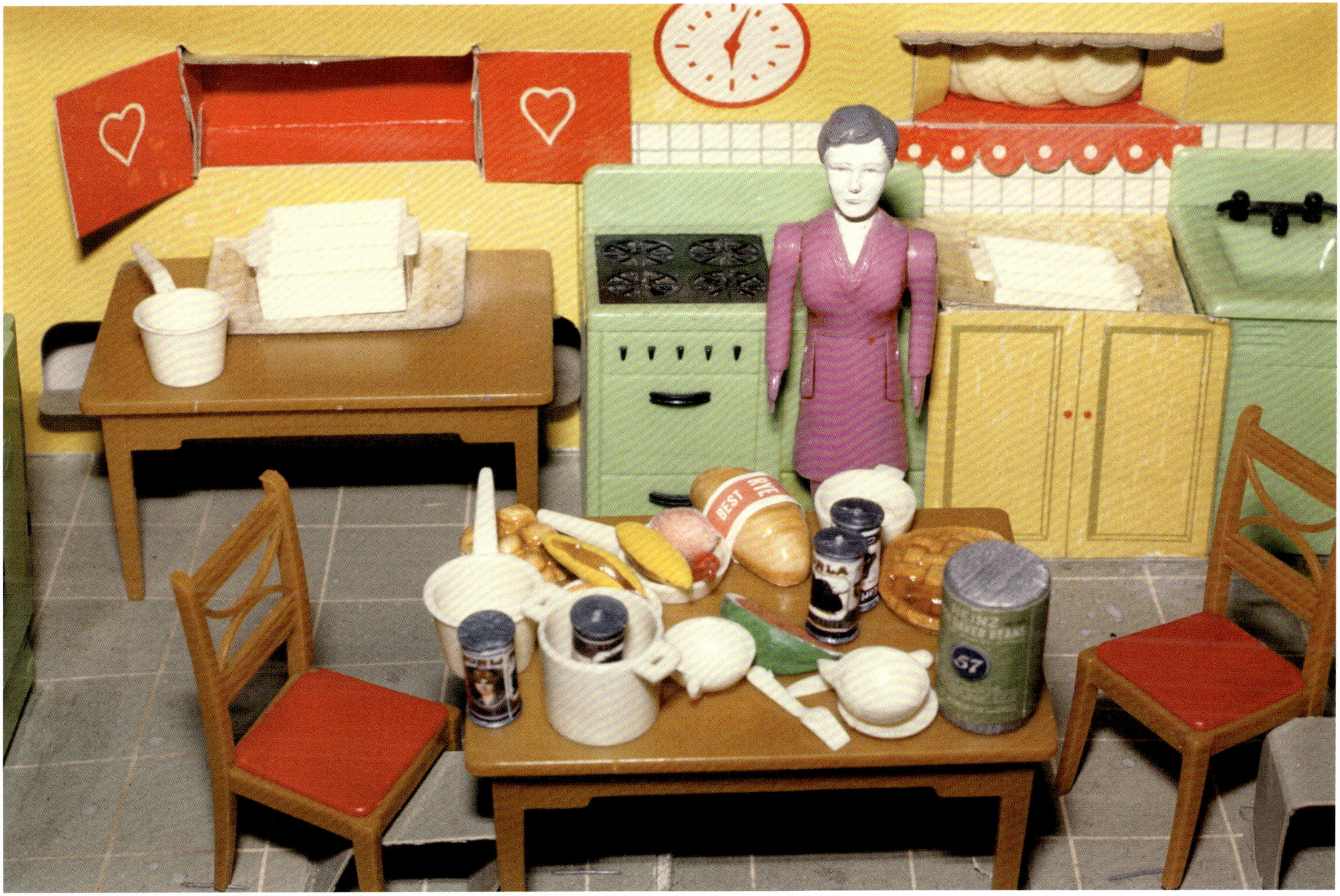
BEST
57

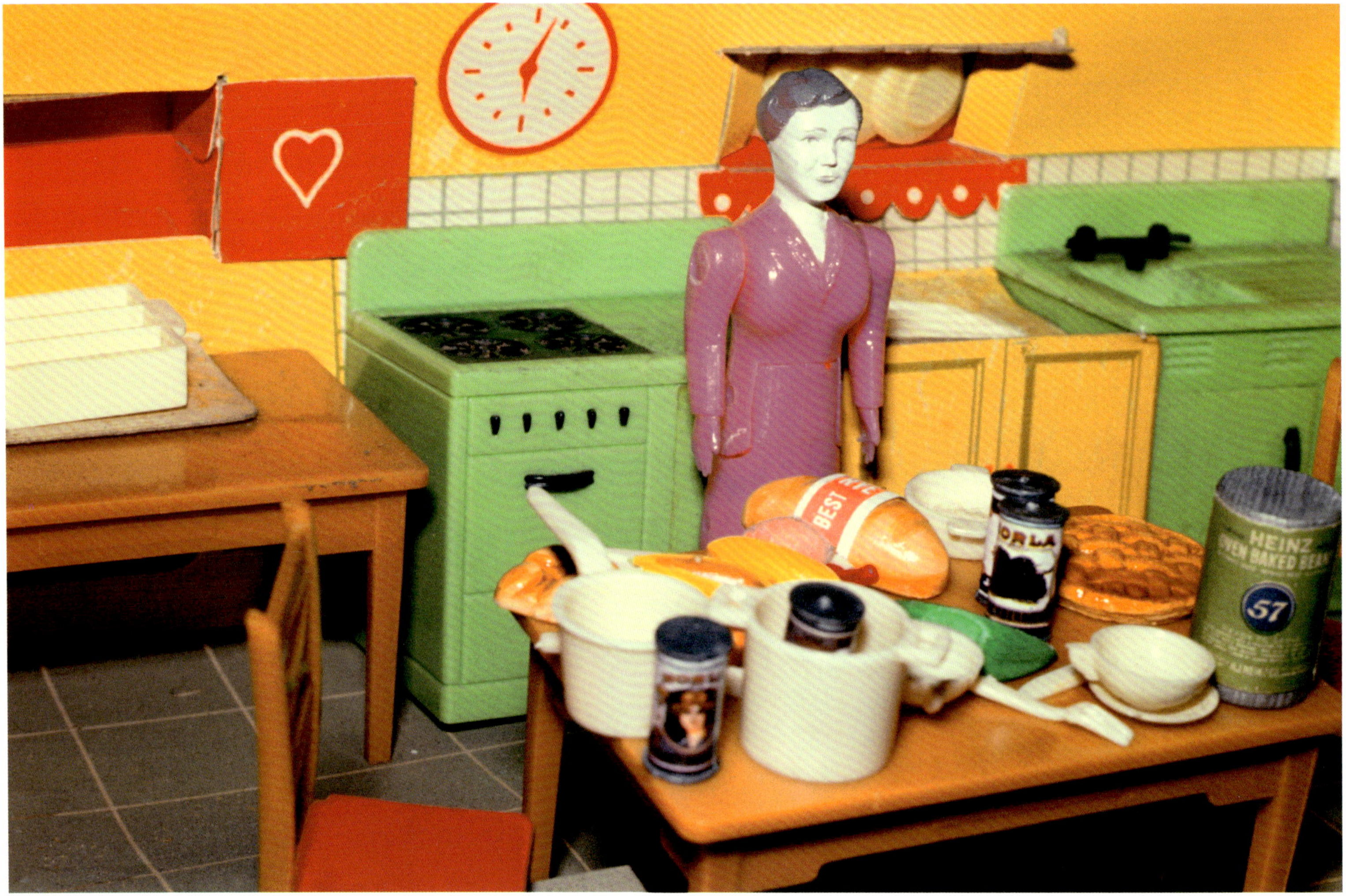
BEST
HEINZ
57

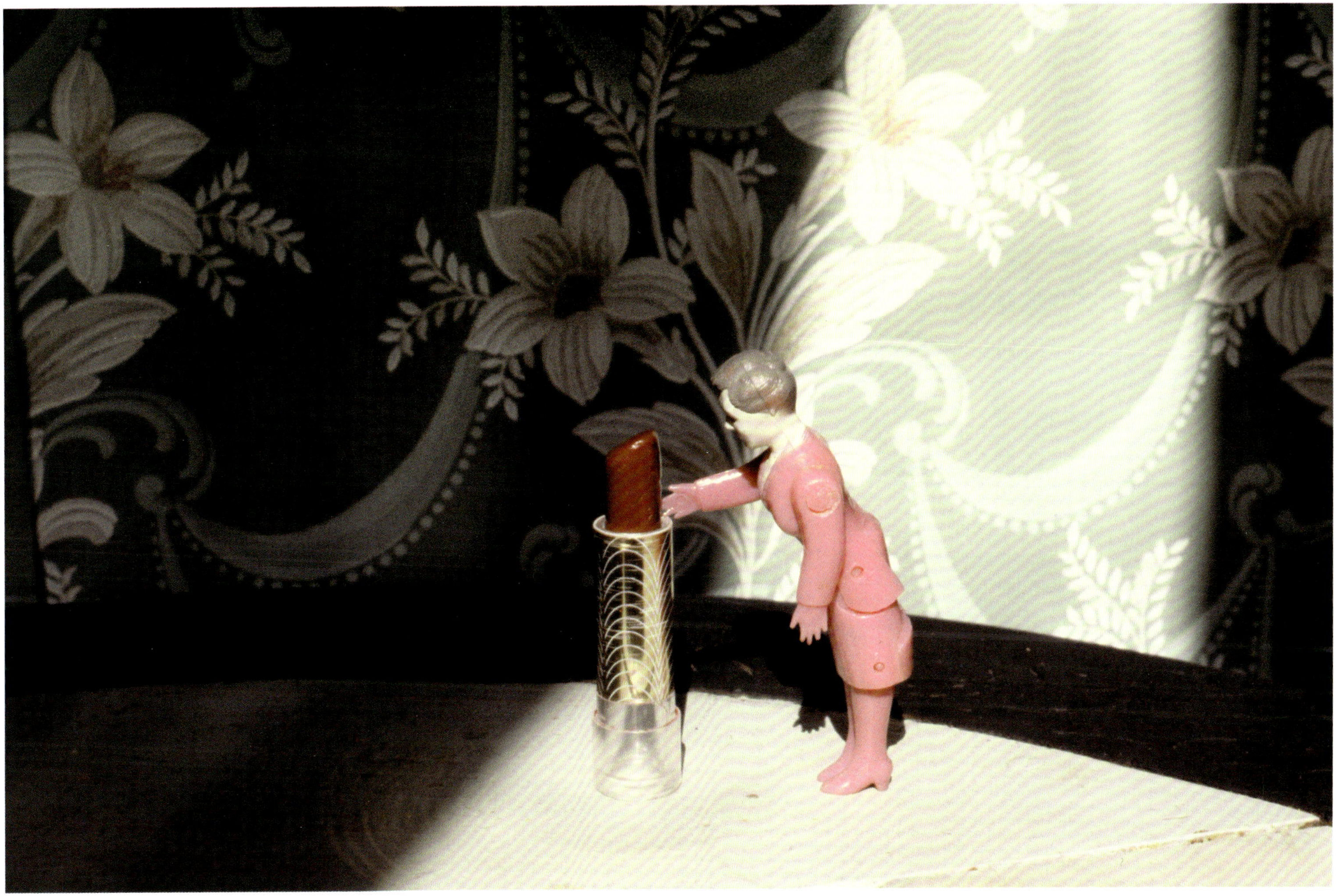

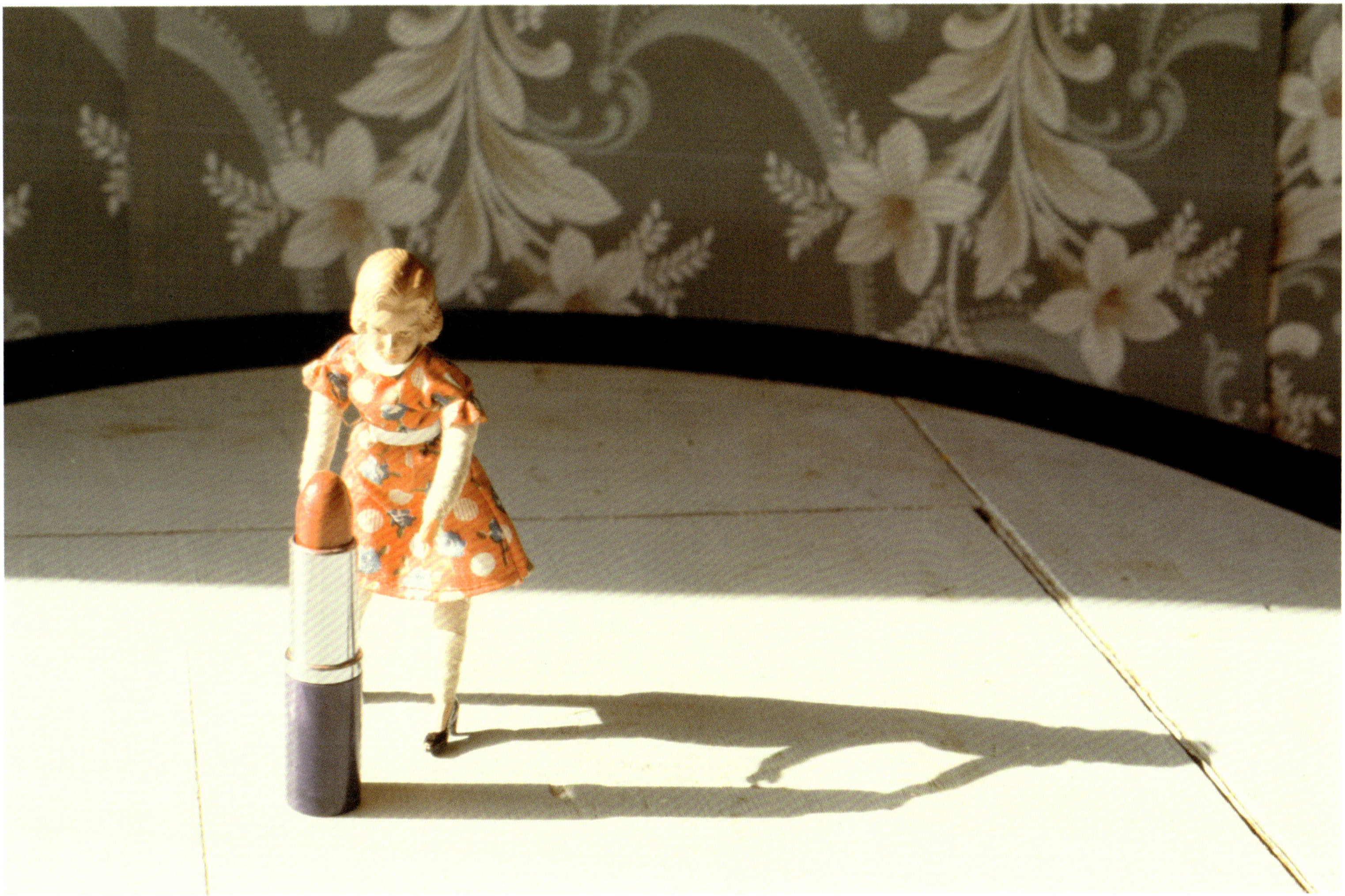

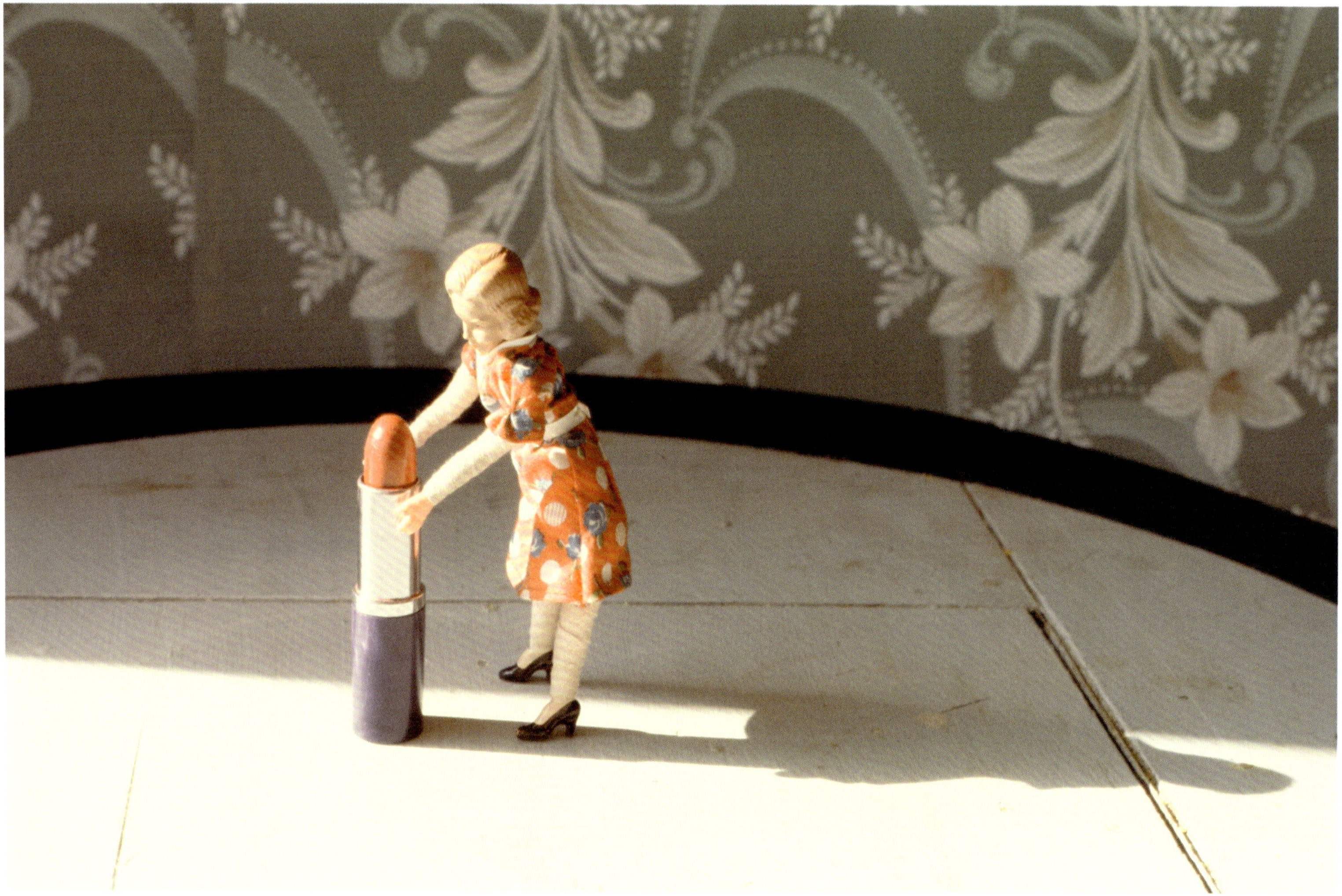

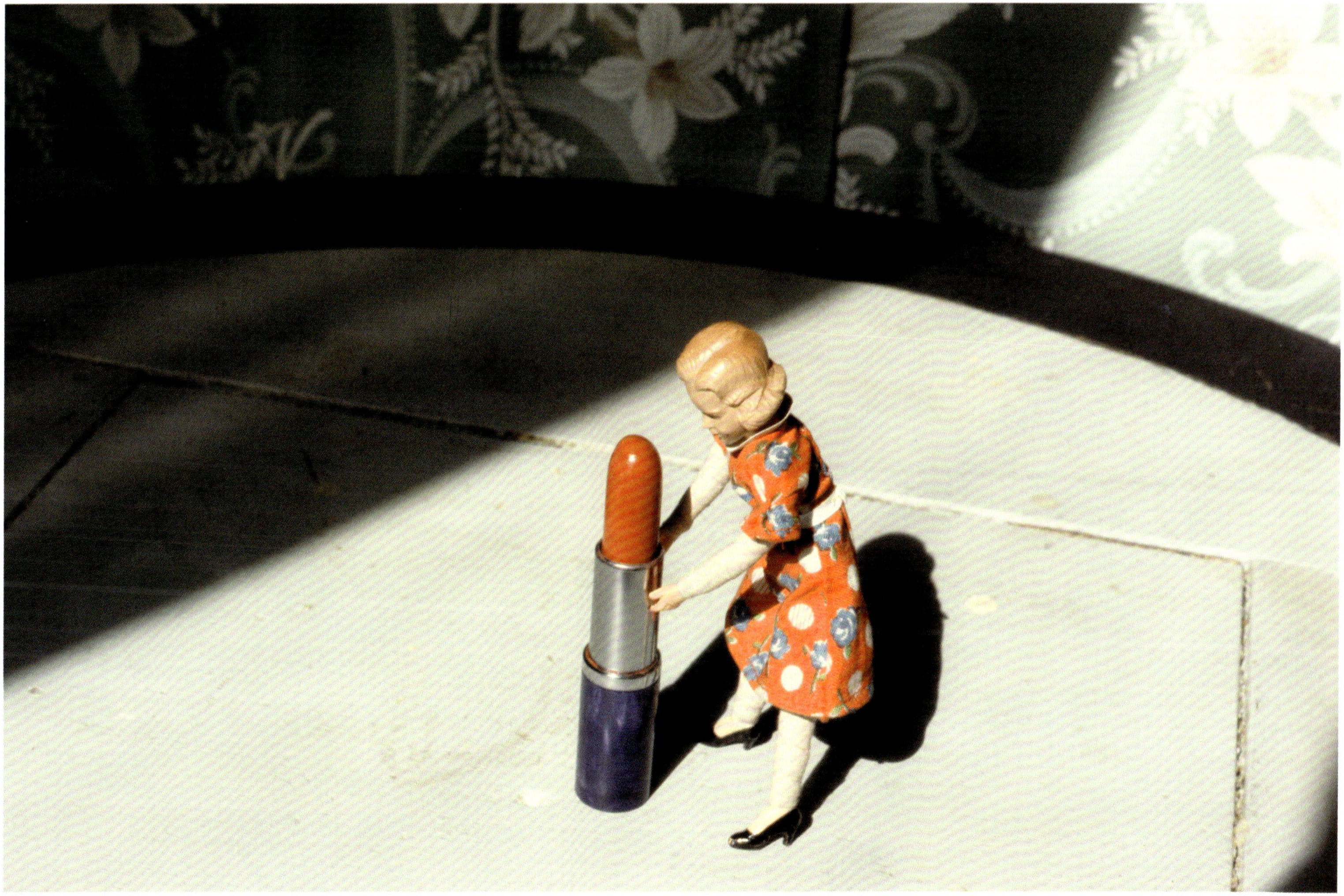

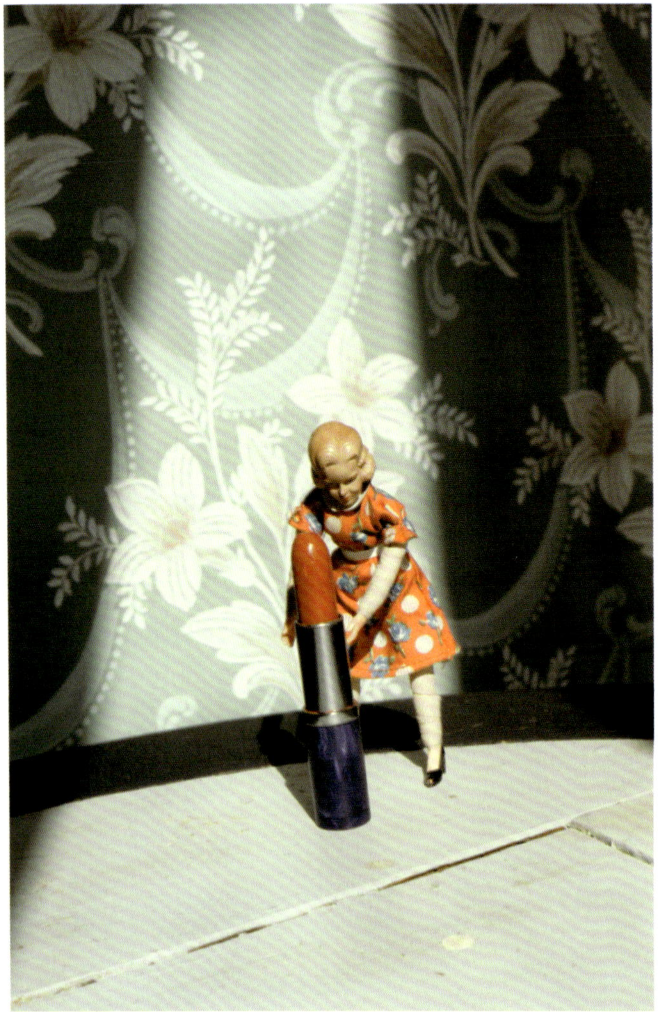

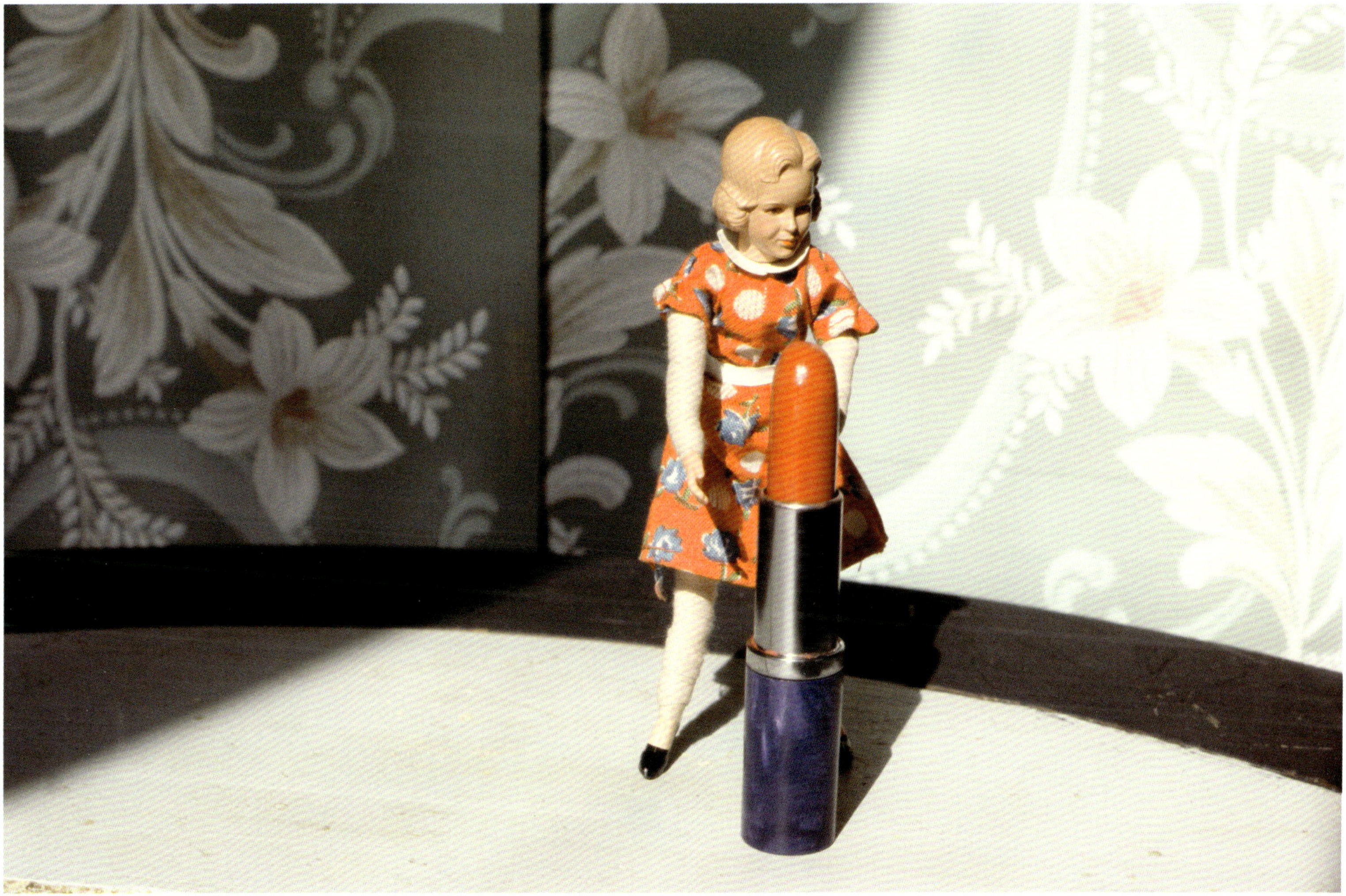

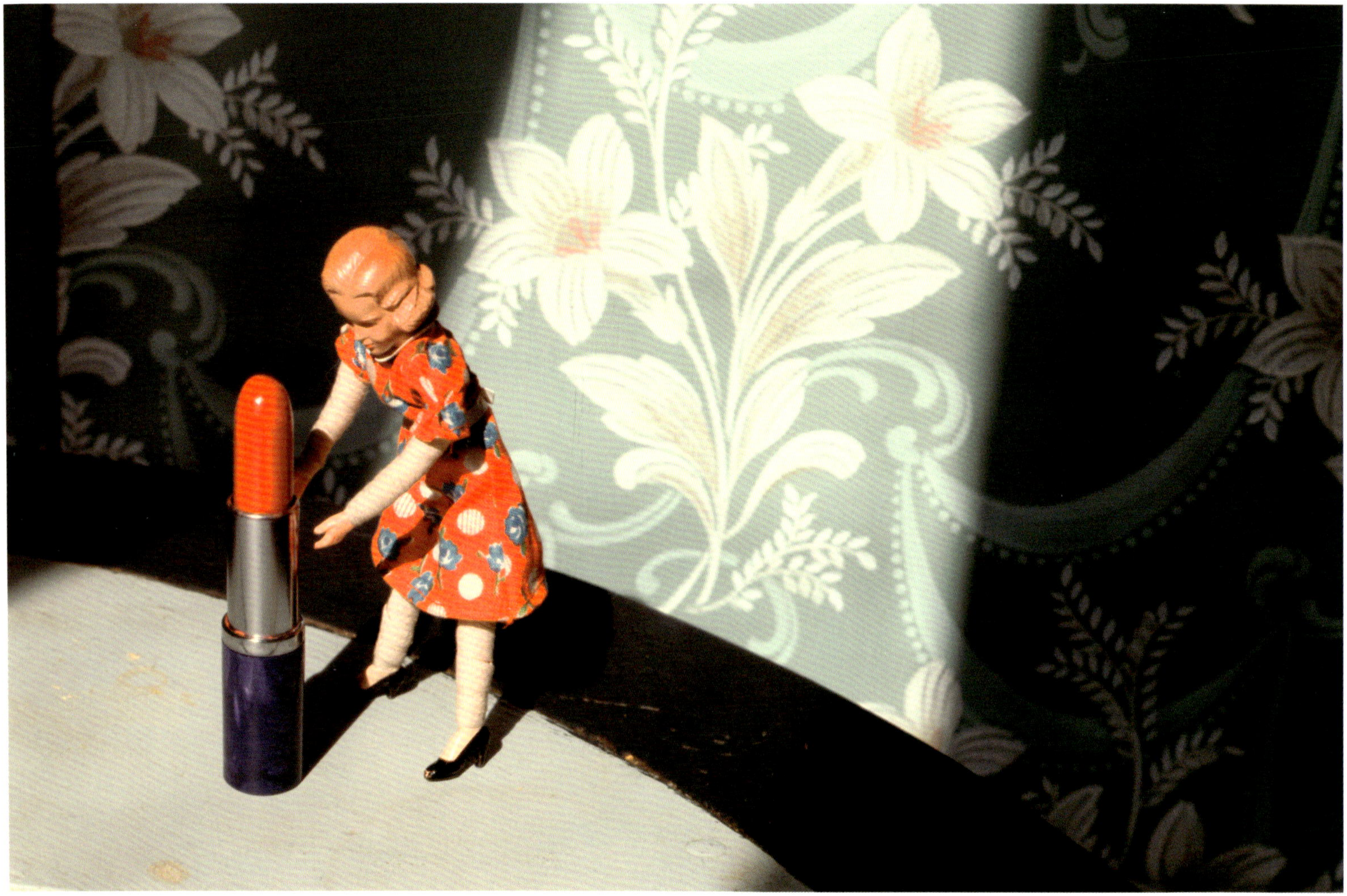

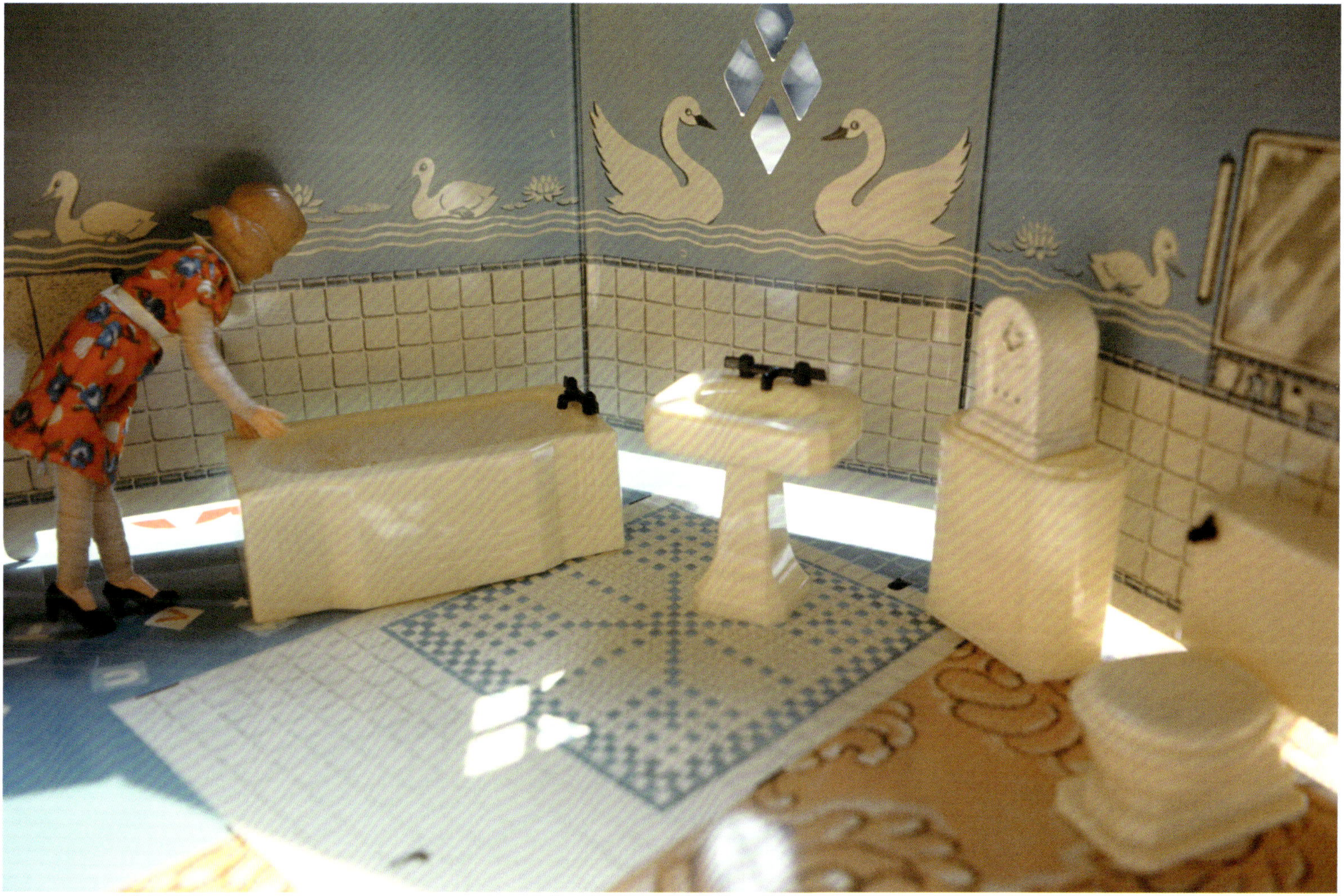

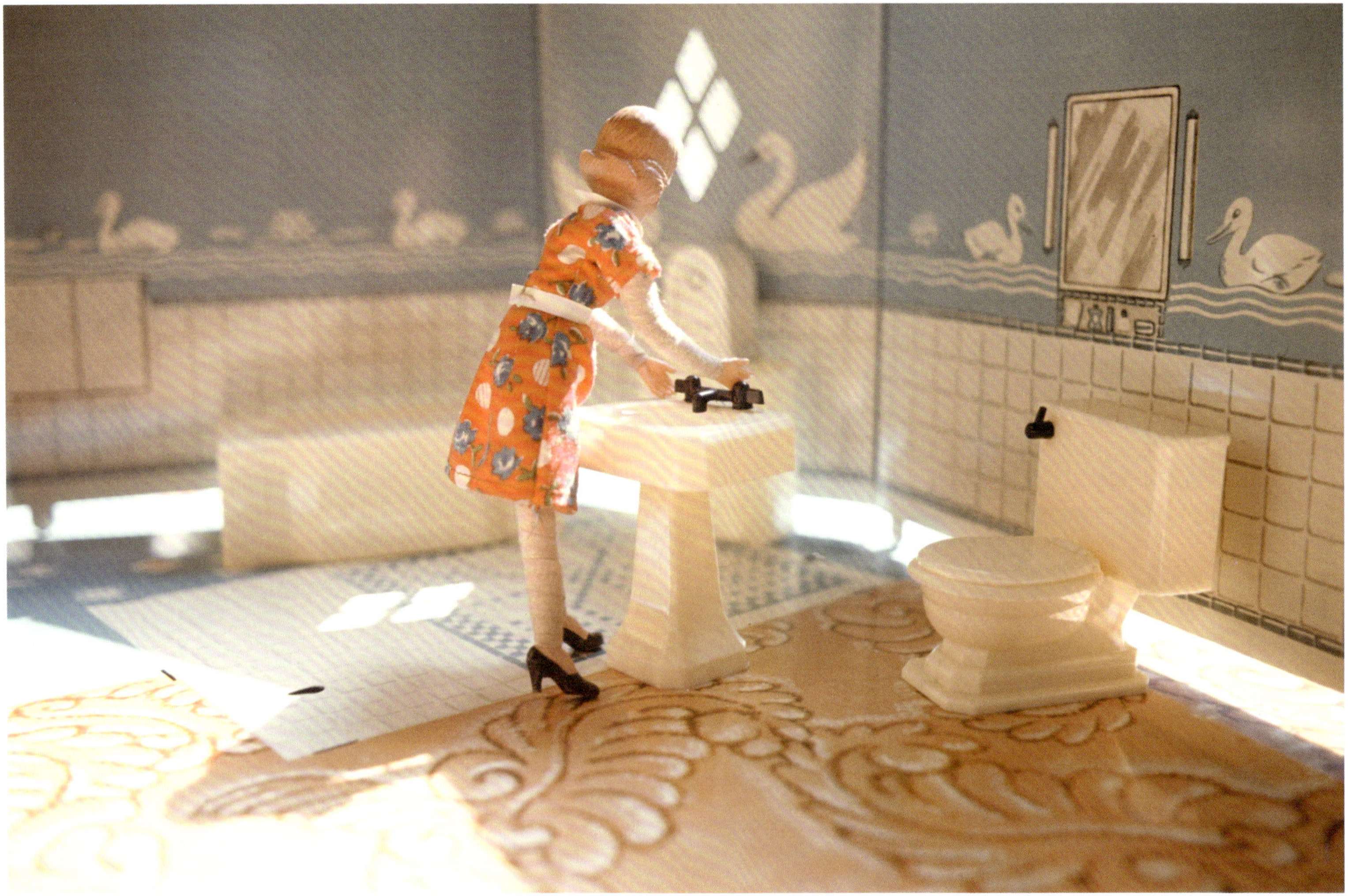

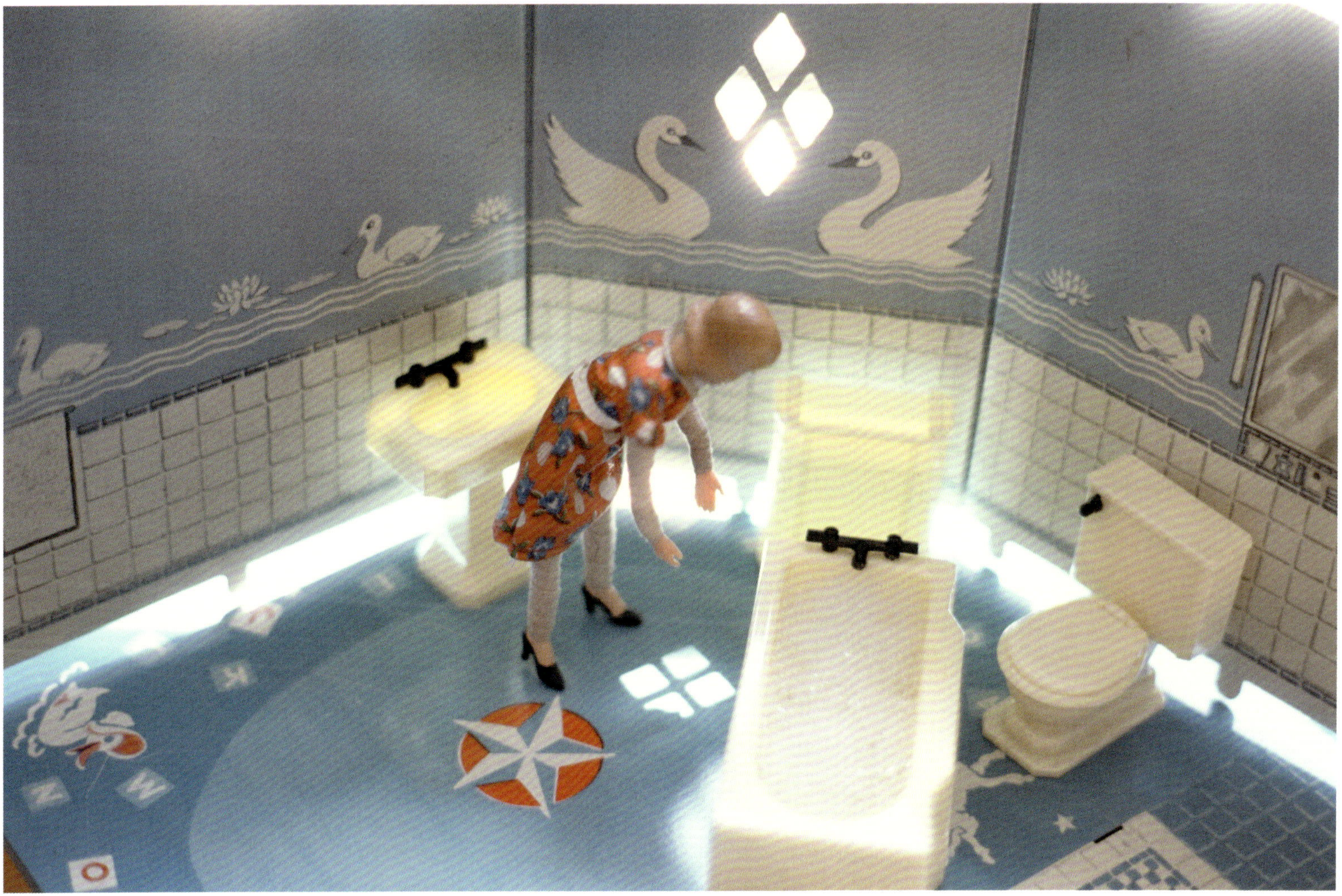

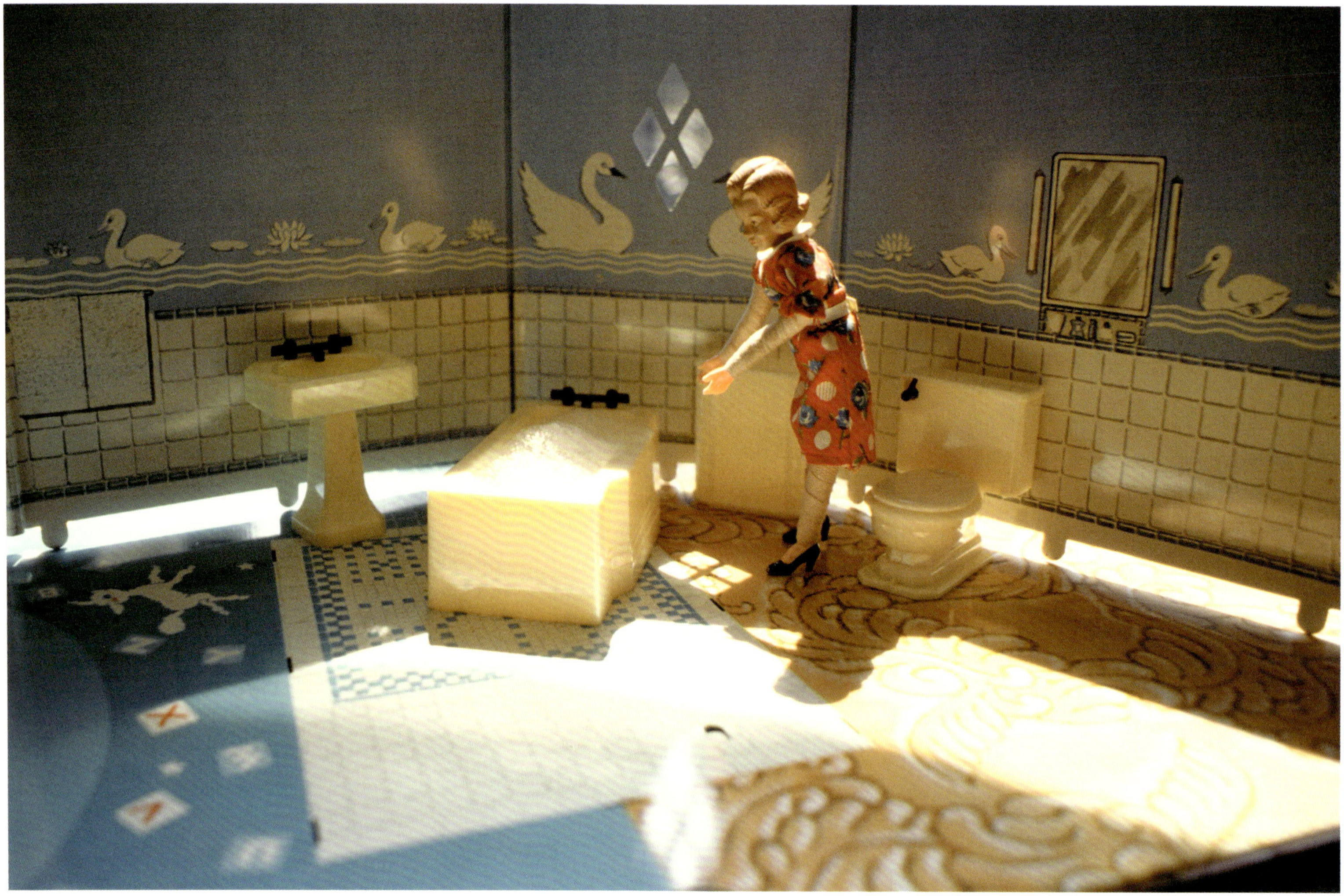

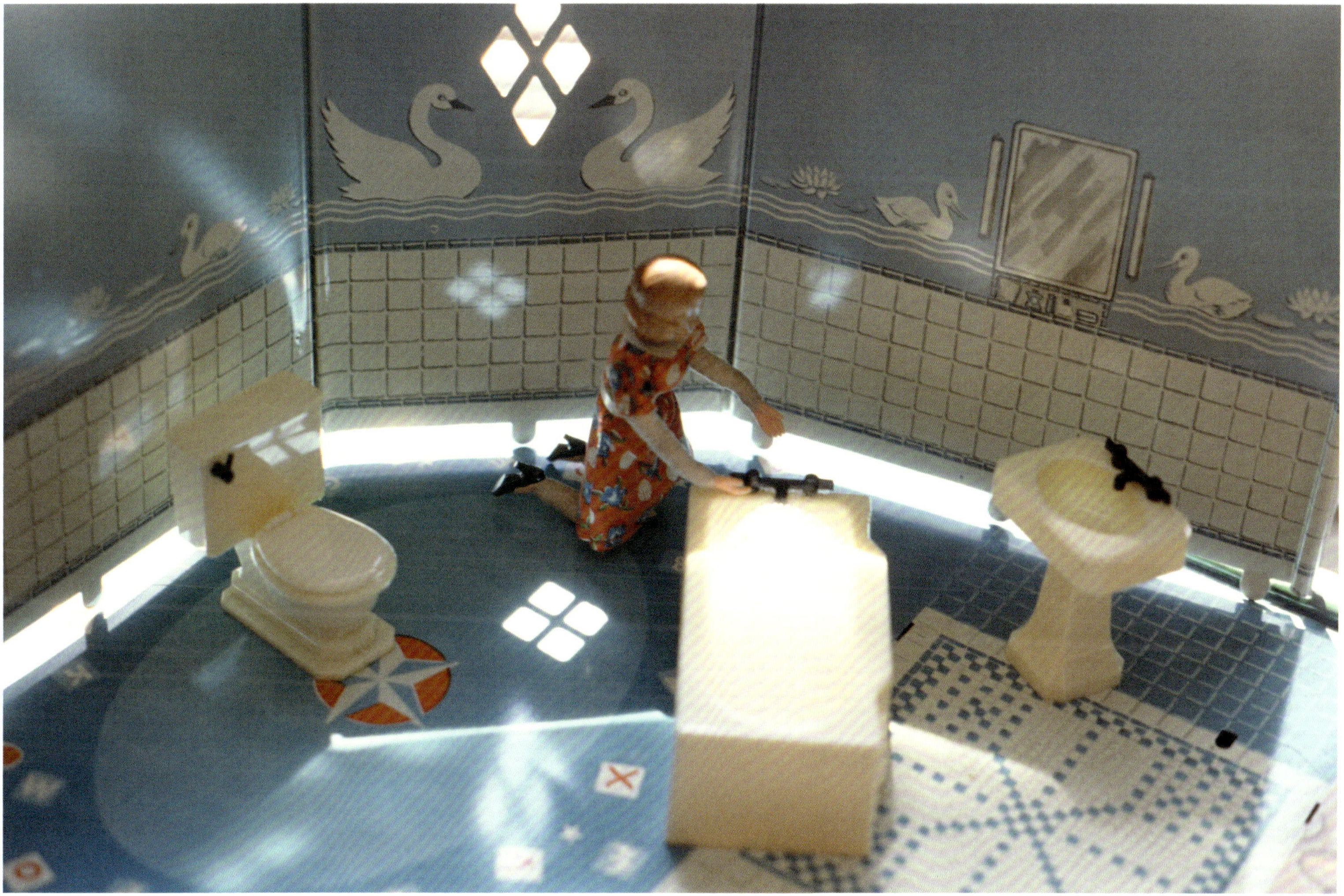

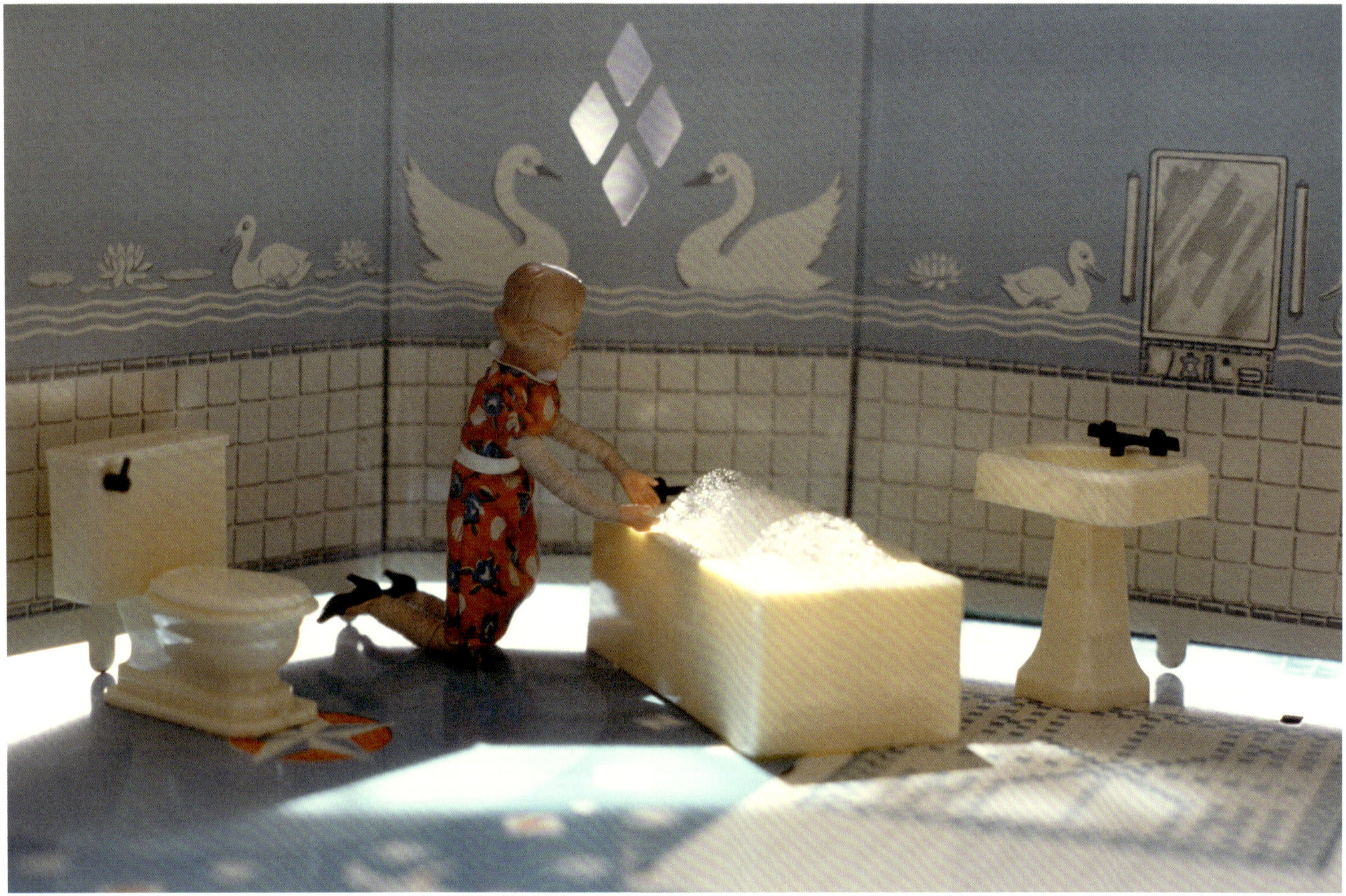

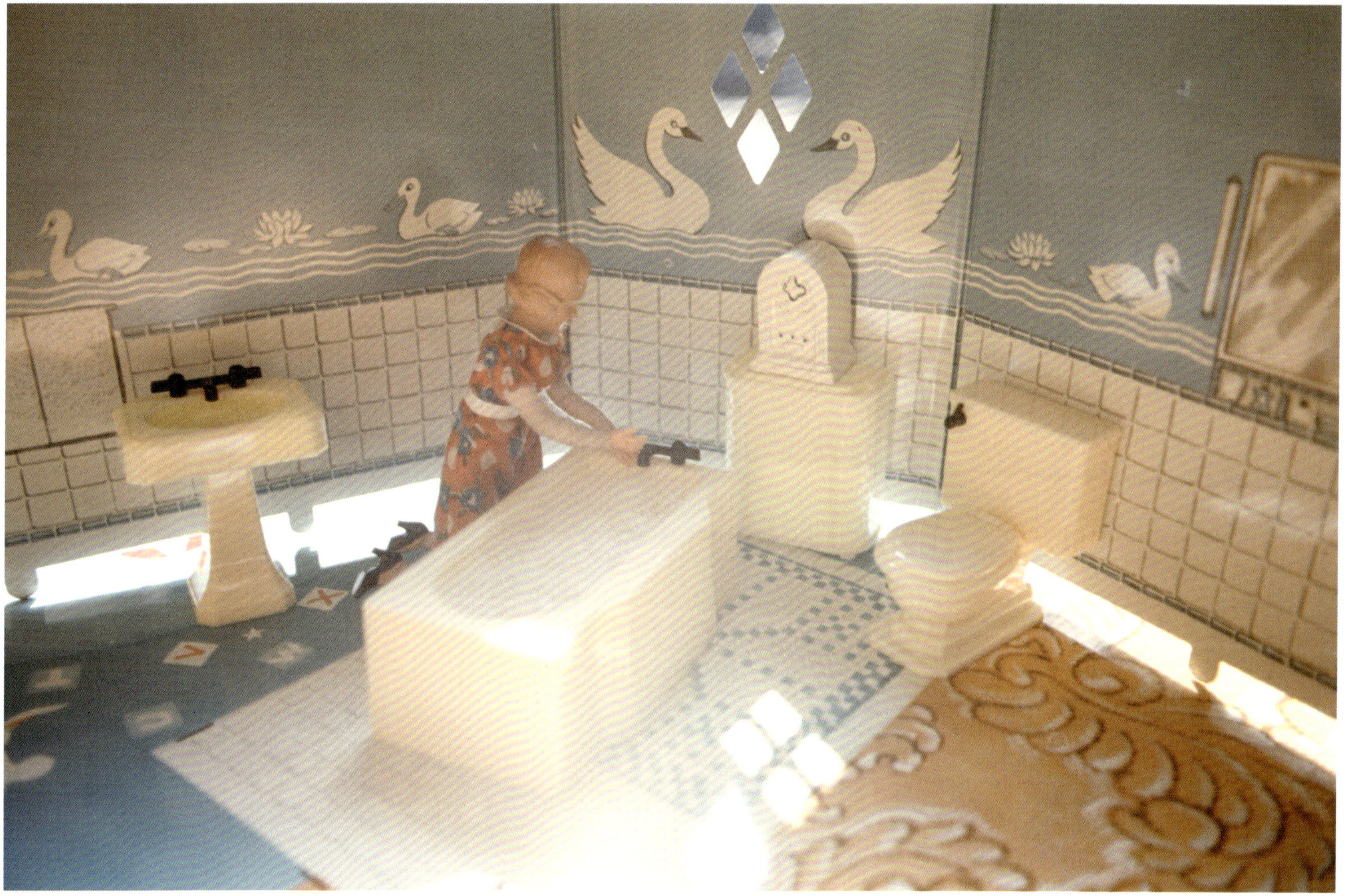

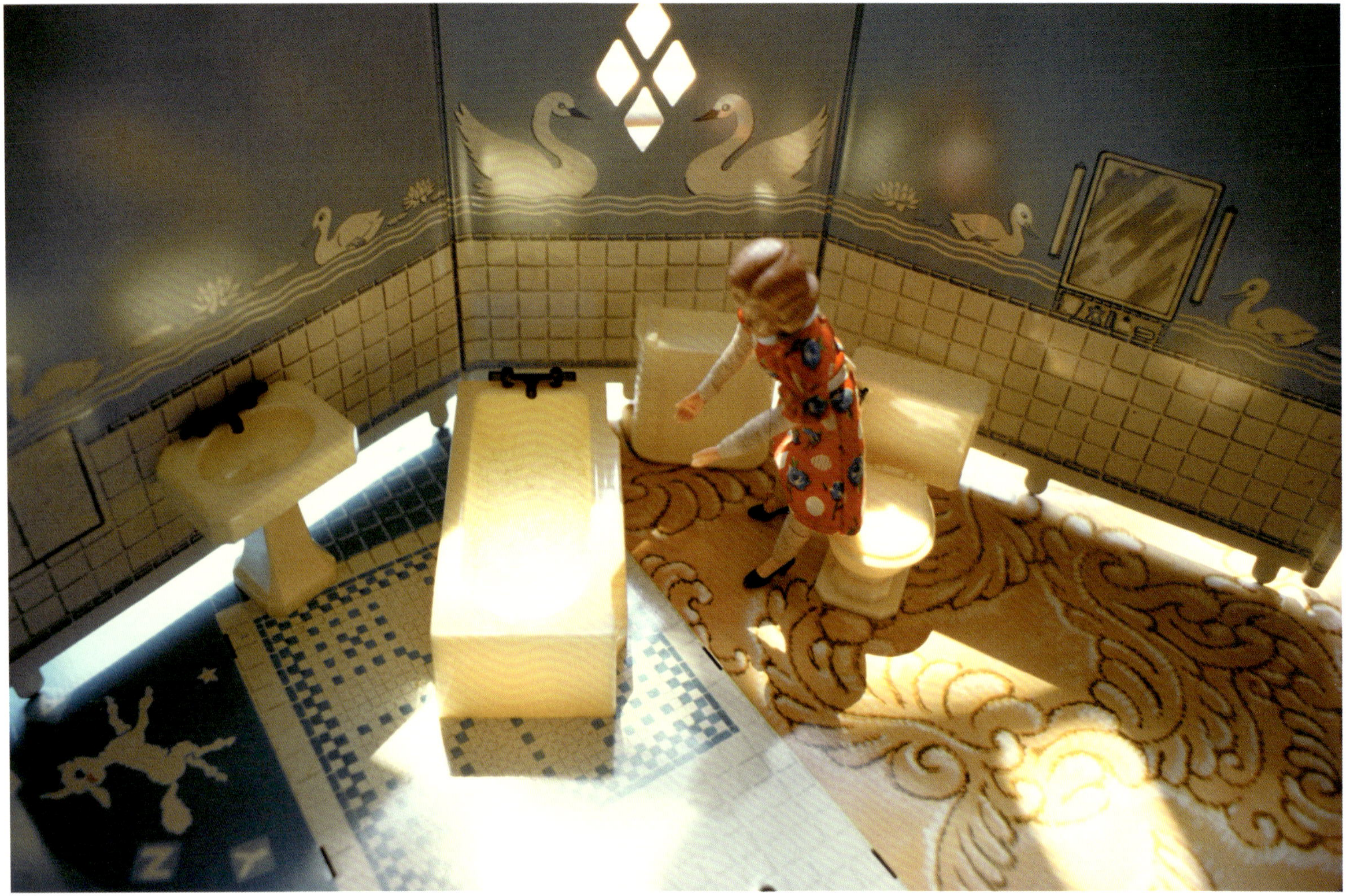

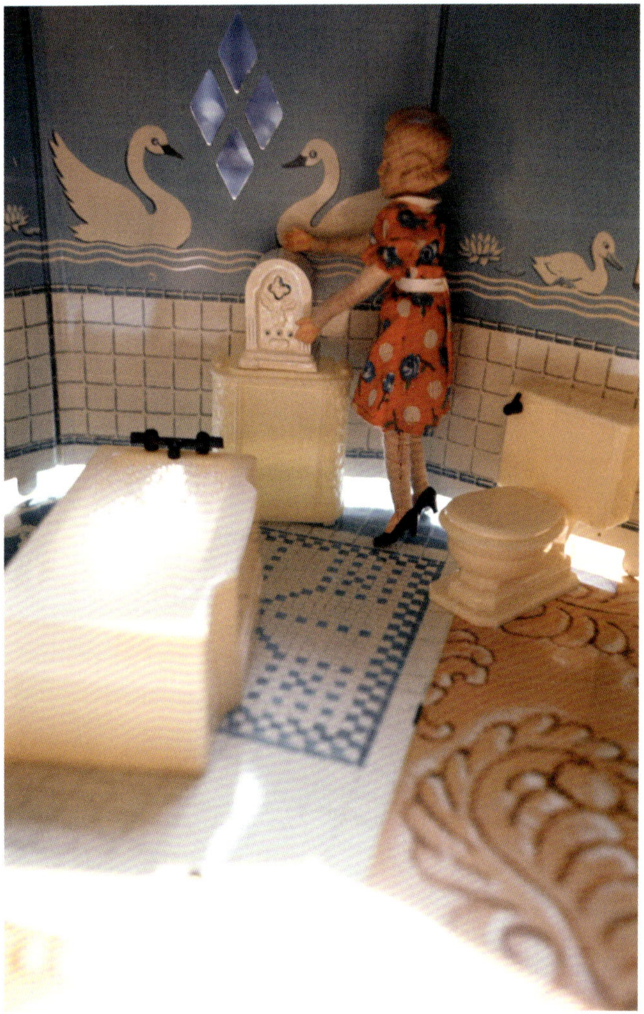

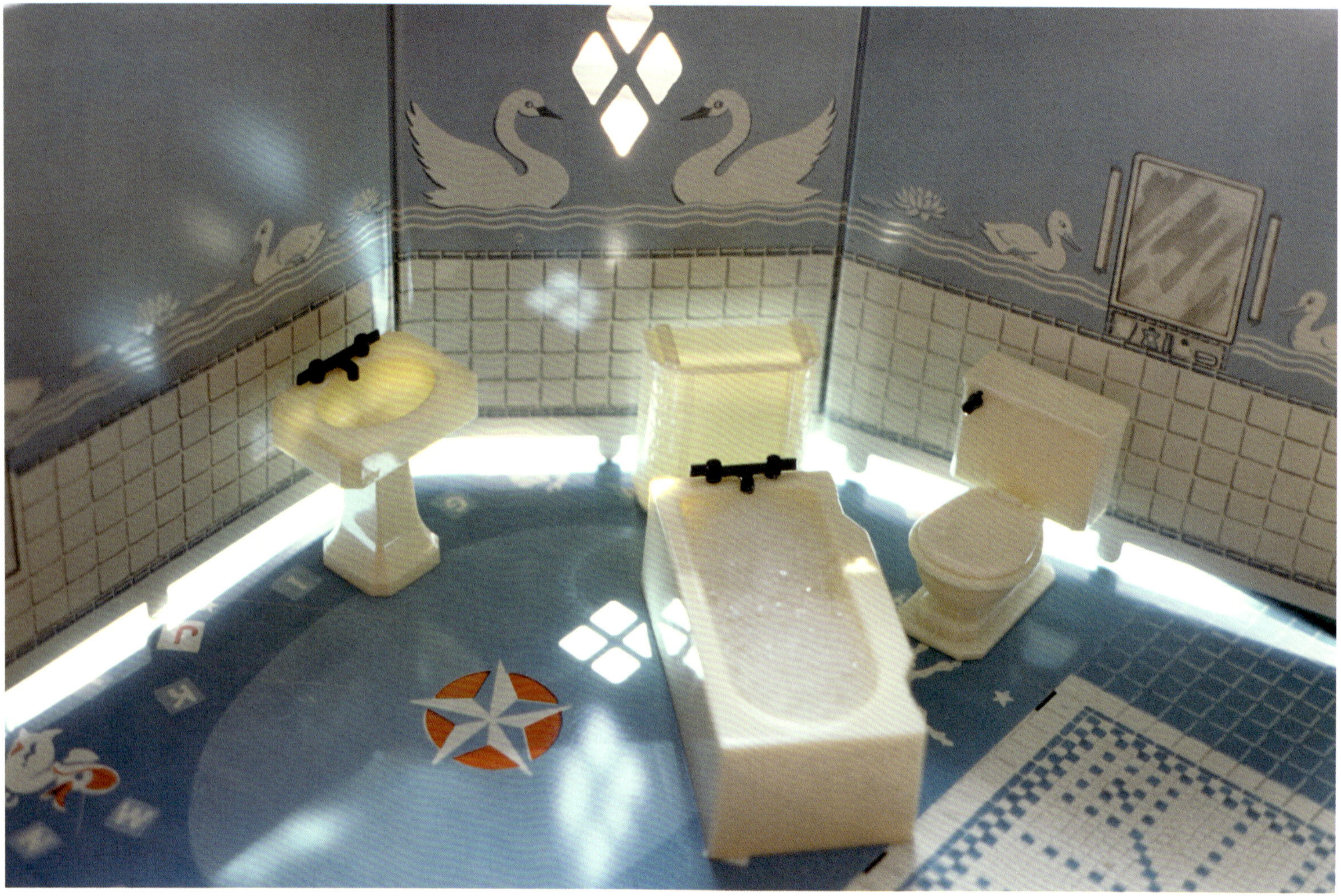

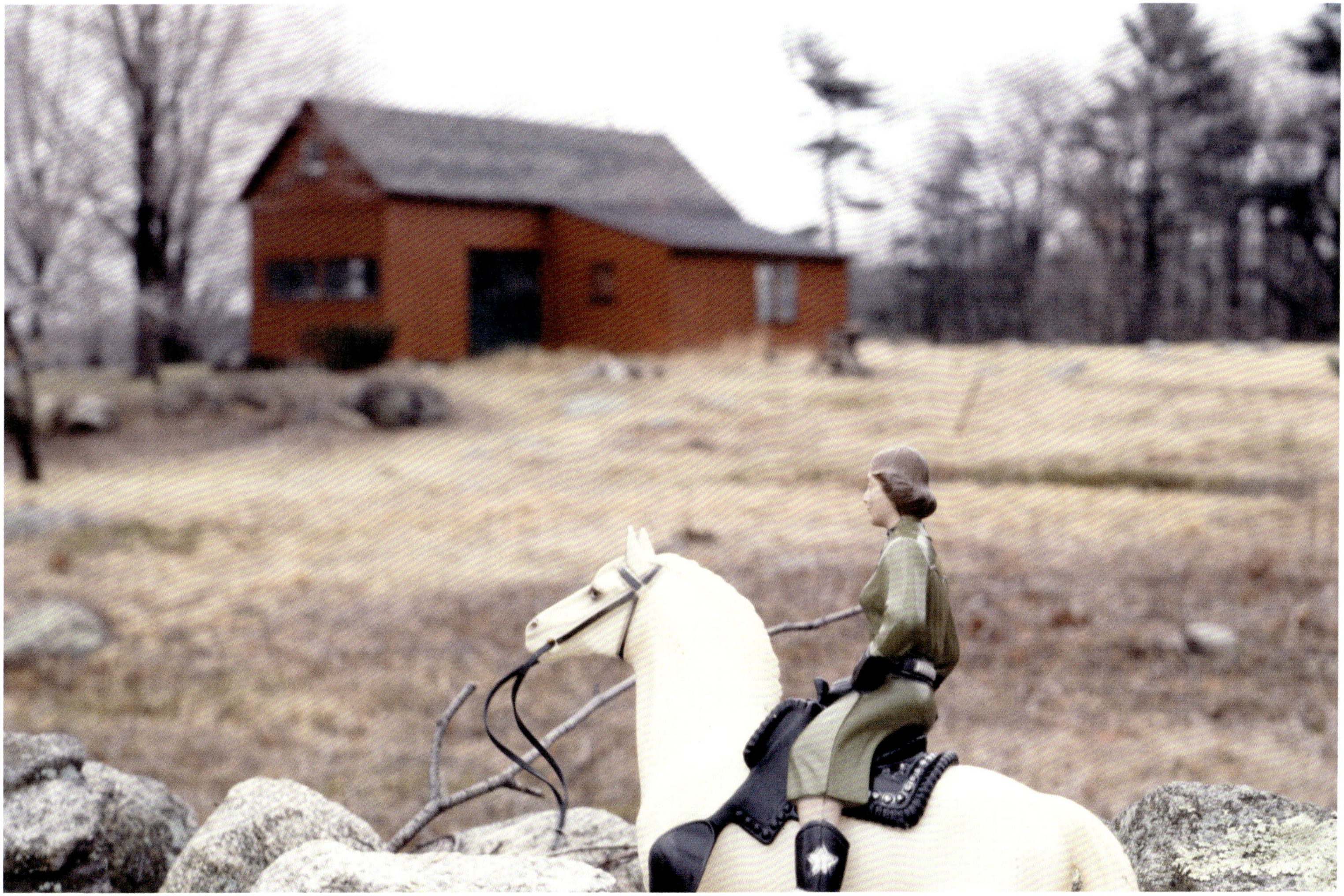

I am a Play, We are all playing now

by **COLLIER SHORR**

Nobody seemed to mind when Gena Rowlands sat in their backyard. When she was in her own front yard crying or hugging her husband John Cassavettes it was a bit disconcerting; lots of rough looking men piled in and out of the house. But when they took a break from filming, the actress would often wander across the back yard set and sit in an empty hammock. Or perhaps, drinking something cool, she might sit at the Johanson's brand new patio suite, the wrought iron kind that was supposed never to rust. It was such a beautiful suite, with six chairs, a side table and something in-between a side table and an ottoman; although one night the neighbors all agreed that a wrought iron ottoman wasn't so inviting.

Gena Rowlands chain smoked, as did all the woman on the block. From behind, with her hair blown out but slightly mussed from so much acting, she looked like everybody else. The actress smoked Pall Malls. Her neighbours on both sides smoked Evergreen 120s. During the second week of shooting Gena Rowlands befriended Pam Steaver. Both woman were from the Midwest. They both had the same way of saying "Well, you know... , " leaning their heads to the right, delivering the second part of the sentence with a puff of smoke. Pam was prettier. Less masculine the neighbours decided. Pam's husband Bob was in insurance, which became a problem socially when he had run through all the potential clients on the block and then refused to host anymore cocktail parties.

So it was not unusual to see the film star napping in the shade of the Steavers's giant willow, sprawled across their bright red chaise lounge, her drink sweating beads of water onto a Japanese coaster Bob picked up in Honolulu. Her head tilted so, with stage lipstick and eyeliner, she looked like a beauty mannequin from a department store window. That's what one of the neighbours said as he and his brother filled their above-ground pool.

The fact of the matter was that although Pam Steaver was a nice person and pretty as could be, Gena Rowlands was hanging around for a very specific reason. She was interested in the way that the Steaver boy's illness was affecting his parents. He had come home from school one day and decided never again to leave his room. At first his parents thought it was a prank or drugs. Rebellion. After all, he had listened to The Ramones *I Want to Be Sedated* for four hours once. Wayne Steaver claimed, with utmost sincerity, that he could not get out of bed. He wouldn't shower and dragged himself to the bathroom only when absolutely necessary. He could only eat sandwiches. This had been going on for a week and while it temporarily turned the Steavers's into the neighbourhood dark cloud, it also made them very appealing to the film people.

The film people were in town making a film, but to the neighbours it seemed more like a play, or a film of a play, like the one they all saw called *Who's Afraid of Virginia Woolf?*; the one that made them all swear off alcohol for one week just to see what would happen. (In the end they agreed that they weren't intellectual enough for the alcohol to make them as deranged as the actors.) The film, starring Gena Rowlands, appeared to be the story of a woman who was having some sort of breakdown. It seemed to involve sex, too. The actress shouted a lot and laughed too loudly.

Her blonde hair was constantly perched in front of her eyes, her hands were always moving, her chin pointing to the sky.
On the first day of filming the neighbours dragged aluminium chairs over to the Mercers and the Hughes to get a better view. It was like a good old- fashioned lawn party. Even the husbands stayed home from work, and the kids didn't have to return to school after lunch. The women made a picnic of cakes and brownies and lemonade that they served to all the actors and technicians. After a few days however, the families stopped coming to the Hughes and the Mercers, or across the street to the McCarthys. As much as they were thrilled to have Hollywood people in Cricketteer Valley they found the theme a little depressing. Perhaps this was because there was something familiar about the way the actress acted or maybe because there wasn't.

Meanwhile, at the Steavers, things were far from improving. Wayne Steaver, a pretty decent cross country runner, hadn't left the house in nine days. Pam Steaver read that if a person didn't wash for ten days the body somehow cleansed itself. Two doctors made house calls. One said the boy had a rare blood disorder. The other said he was momentarily insane, but he could snap out of it at any time and they shouldn't be surprised if he came into their bedroom late at night and said hi. Pam wanted to ask him how not to be surprised if her insane son woke them up in the middle of the night, but then decided any more discussion was pointless. Had anyone thought to check with the local librarian they would have discovered that Wayne had been reading John Cheever's *Bullet Park* just two weeks before he took to bed. Anyone who had read *Bullet Park* would recognize, if not the symptoms, than surely the plot. Rather than experimenting with drugs, Wayne Steaver was exploring his capacity for melancholia. Each day that he spent in bed made him feel lighter than when he dropped acid or ate mushrooms. He was in a trance of wonderful privacy and the house, which never felt one way or the other, suddenly seemed infinitely more commanding. He could hear every movement his mother made when she travelled through its rooms. The ice tea cracking cubes of ice as it filled up a glass, the snap of sheets billowing above mattresses, a sponge lagging against furniture polish, a skirt being smoothed, the sound of magazine pages turning, the interruption of one being torn out. A whole world was alive beneath his bed. His mother was a fascinating creature, whom he would love to get to know, if getting up to greet her wouldn't shatter the melancholic grip that allowed him to finally see her.

Gena Rowlands watched Pam Steaver through the glass sliding doors that led from the patio into the family room. She was vacuuming a throw rug. Sometimes she would stop to move an end table or to pin back a lock of silky yellow hair that always seemed to spill out when she bent too low. She knew the actress was studying her, watching her skirt rise up, waiting to see when she would lose it; a husband in insurance, a comatose son, a plush white rug. She was tempted to crumble to the floor, just to fulfill her voyeur's expectations, but honestly, she herself was waiting for the moment to come and so far, it hadn't. So she continued, trying to make her afternoon as interesting as possible so that the actress wouldn't feel she were wasting her time. Pam wondered if she should invite Gena Rowlands inside. She felt like a bad host, going to clean the bathroom while the actress sat unattended in the backyard.

Collier Schorr

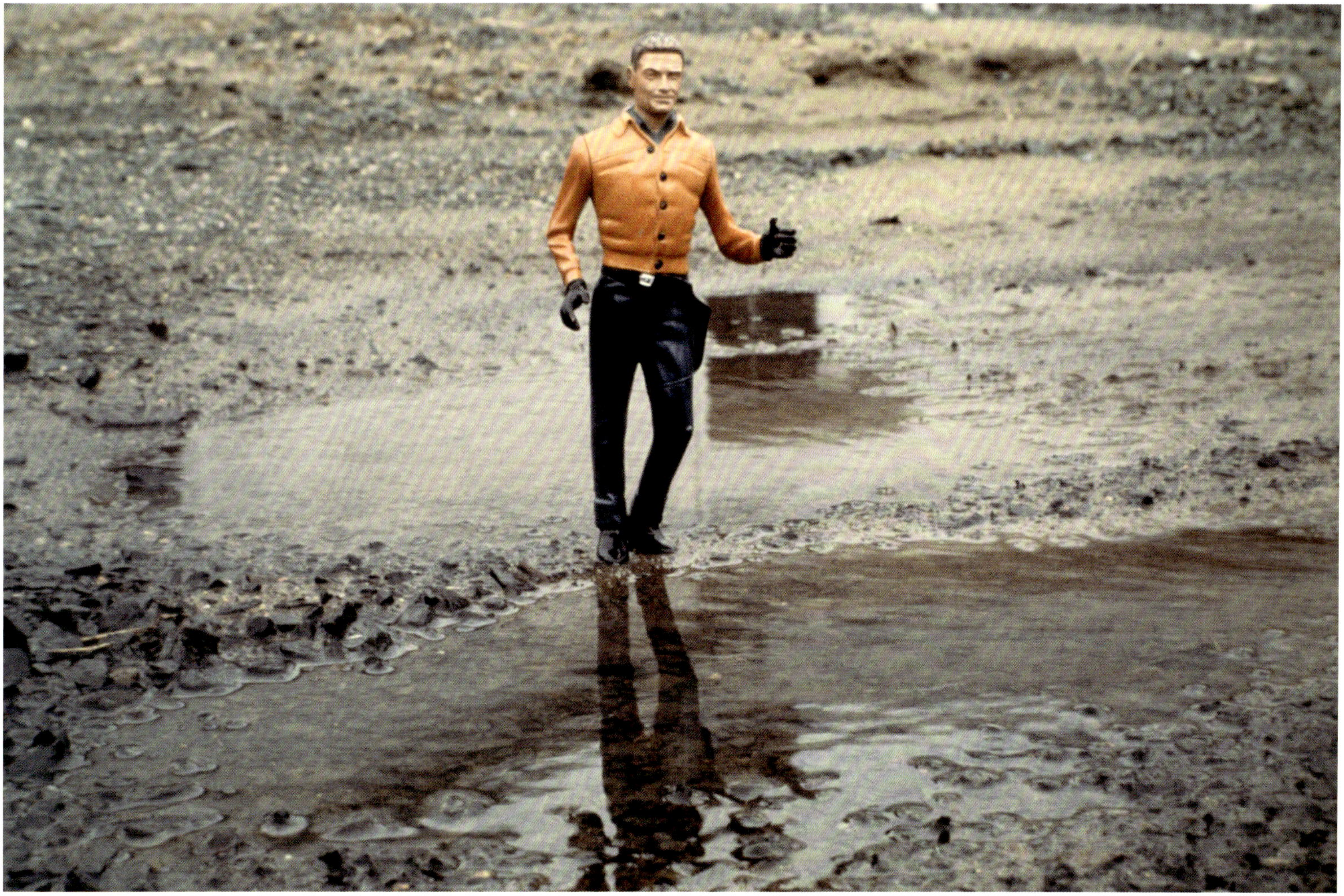

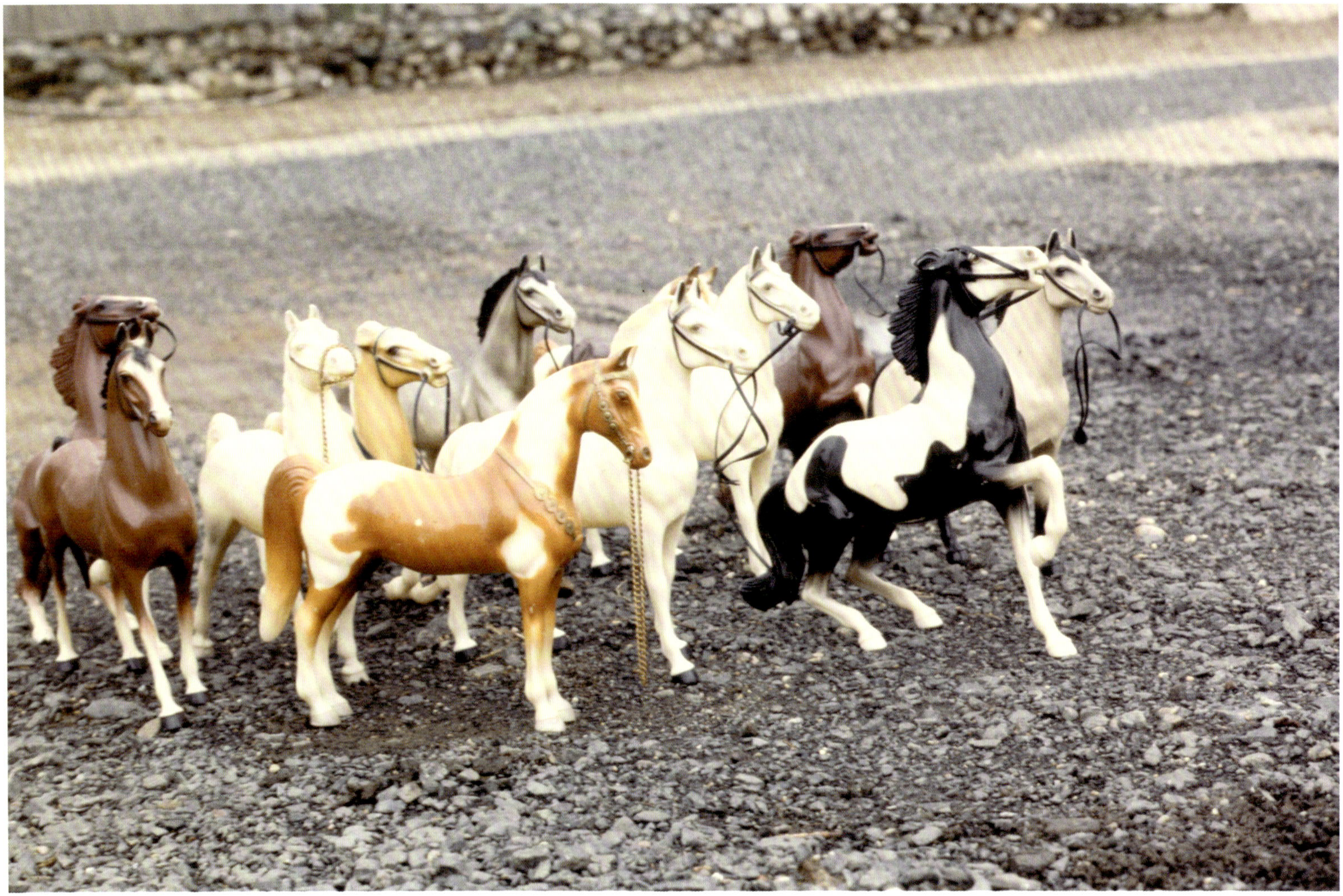

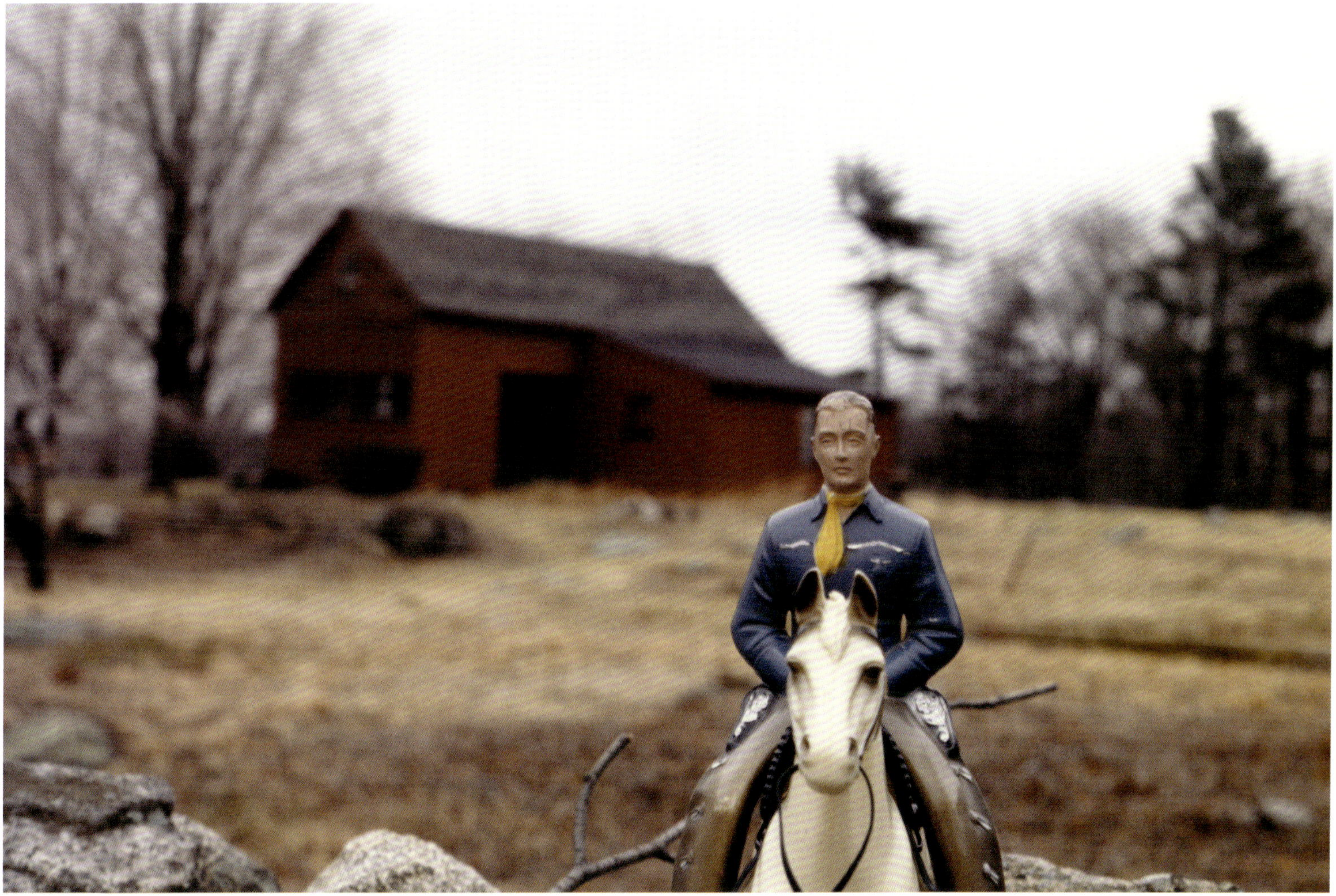

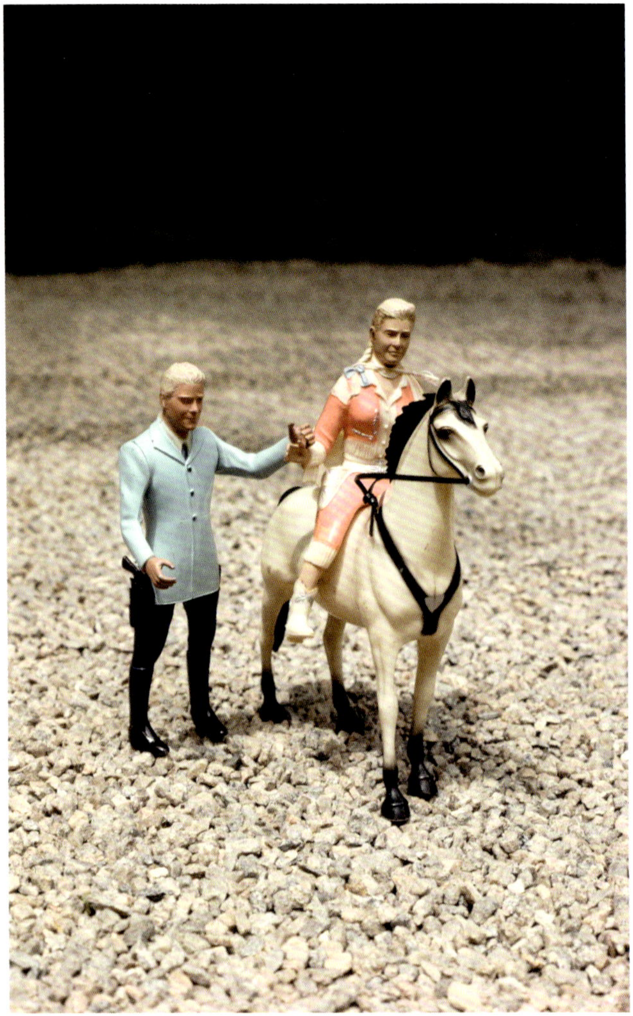

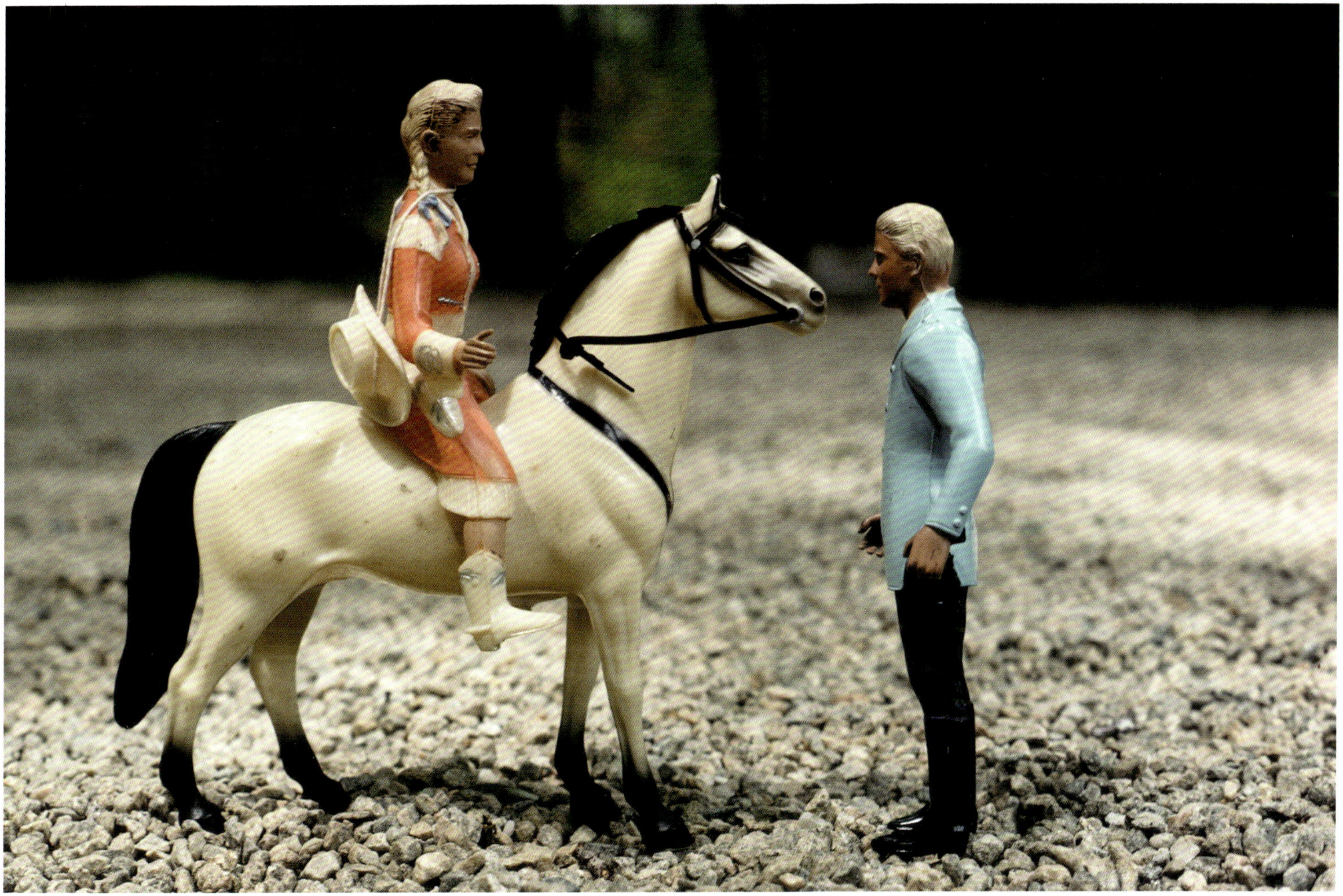

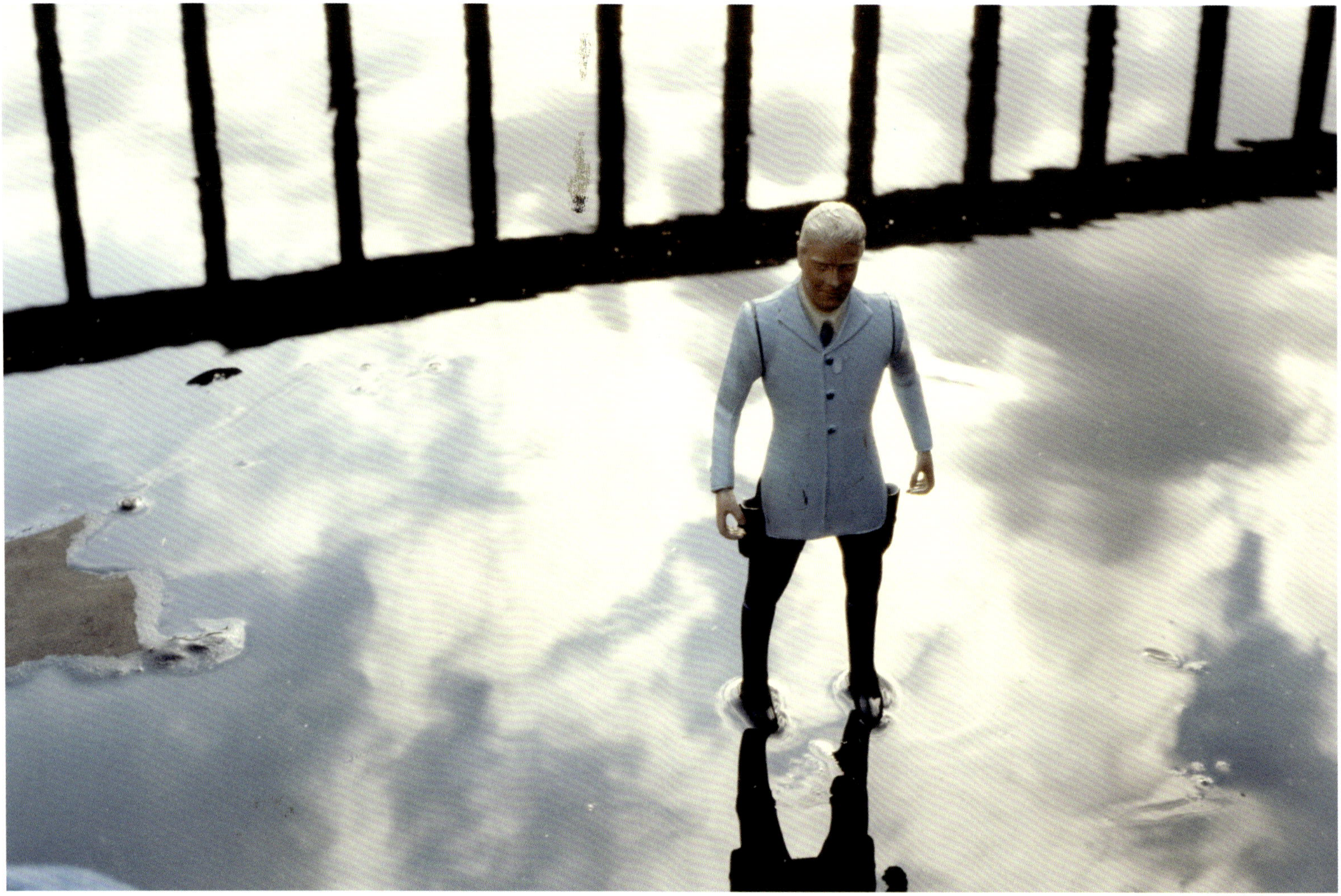

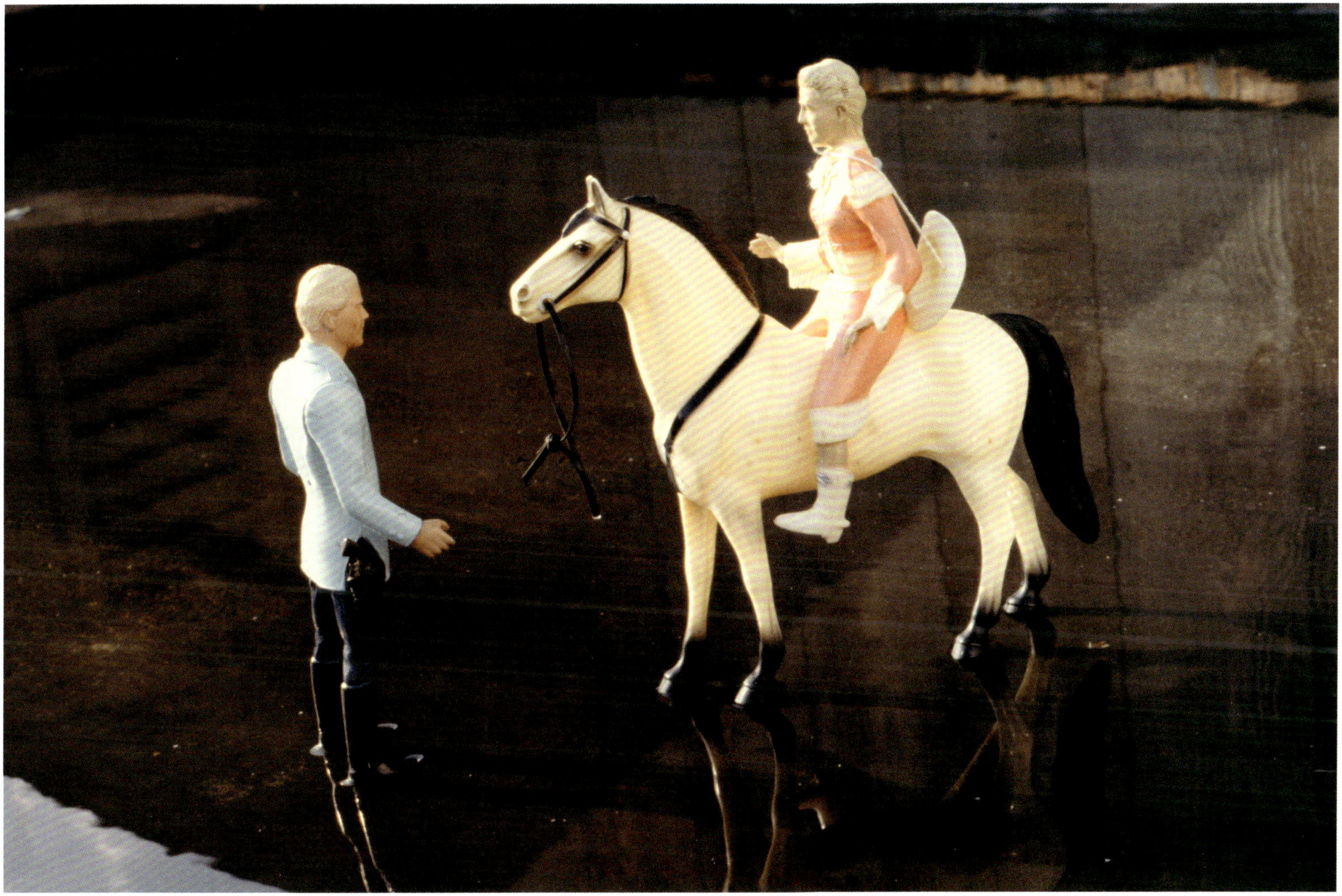

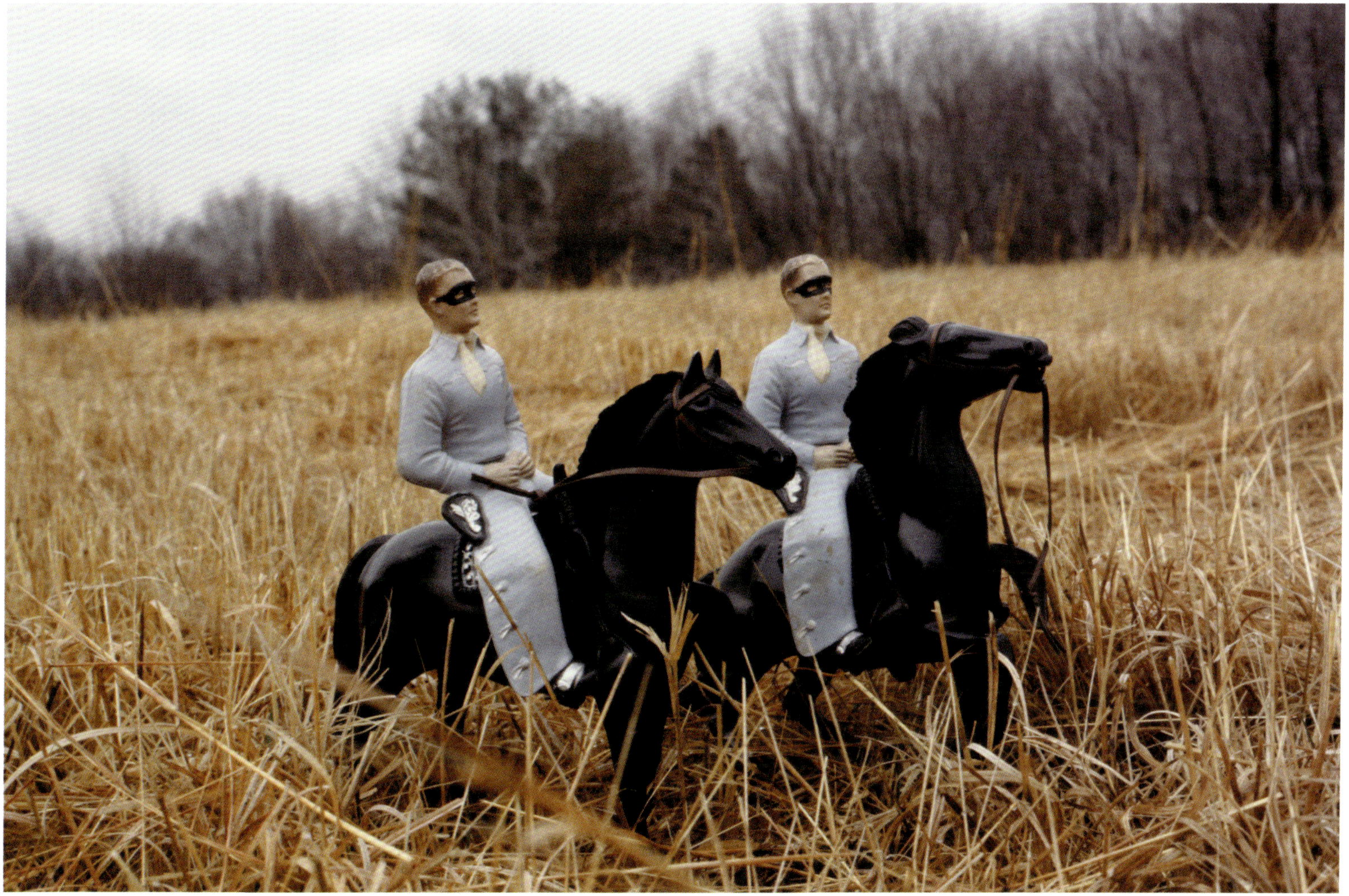

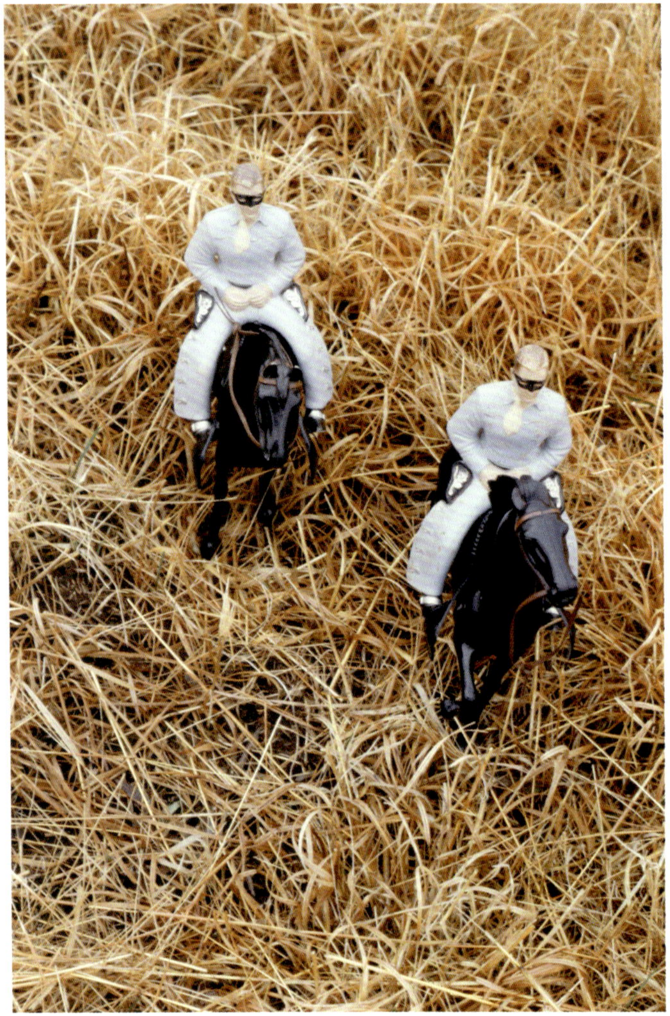

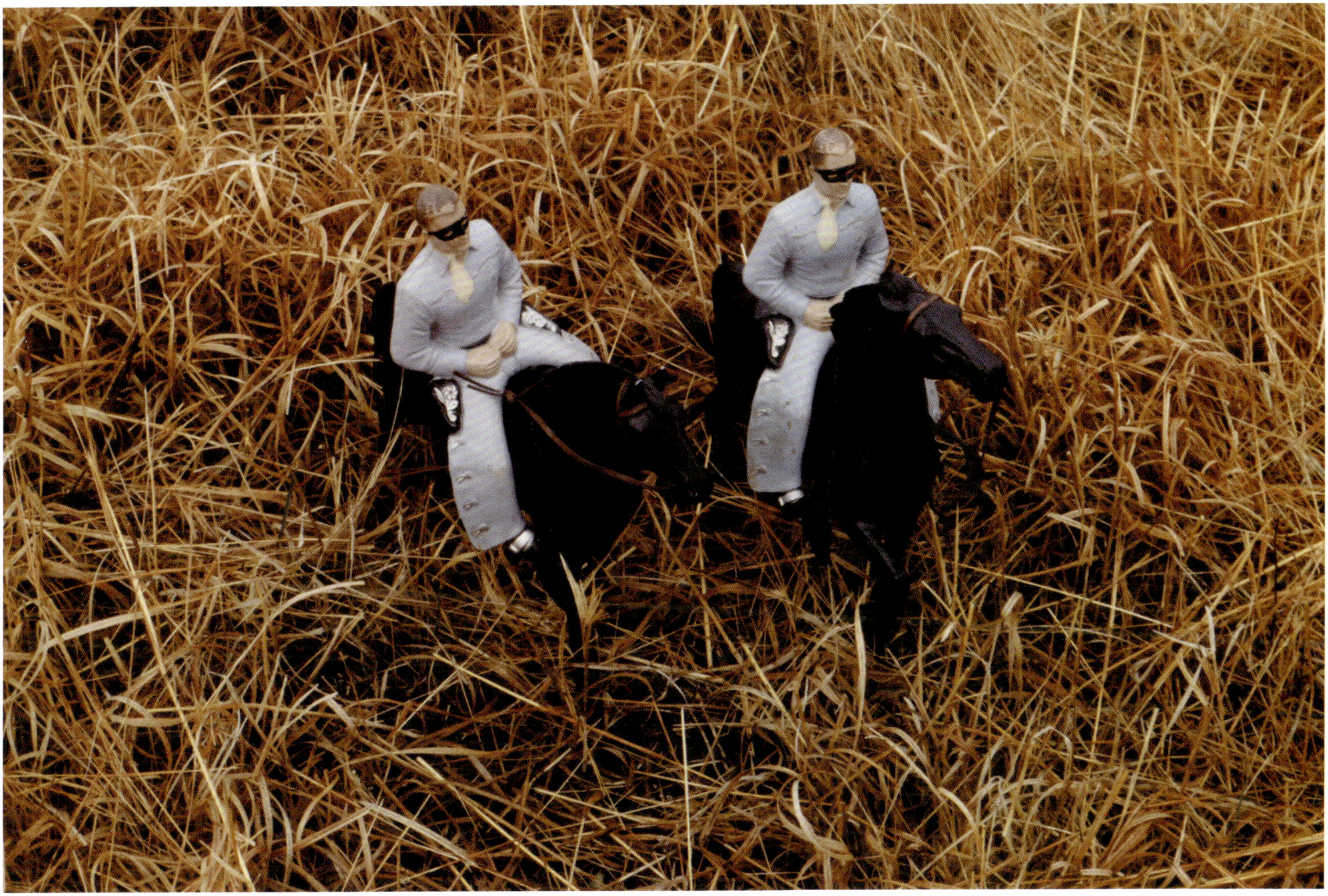

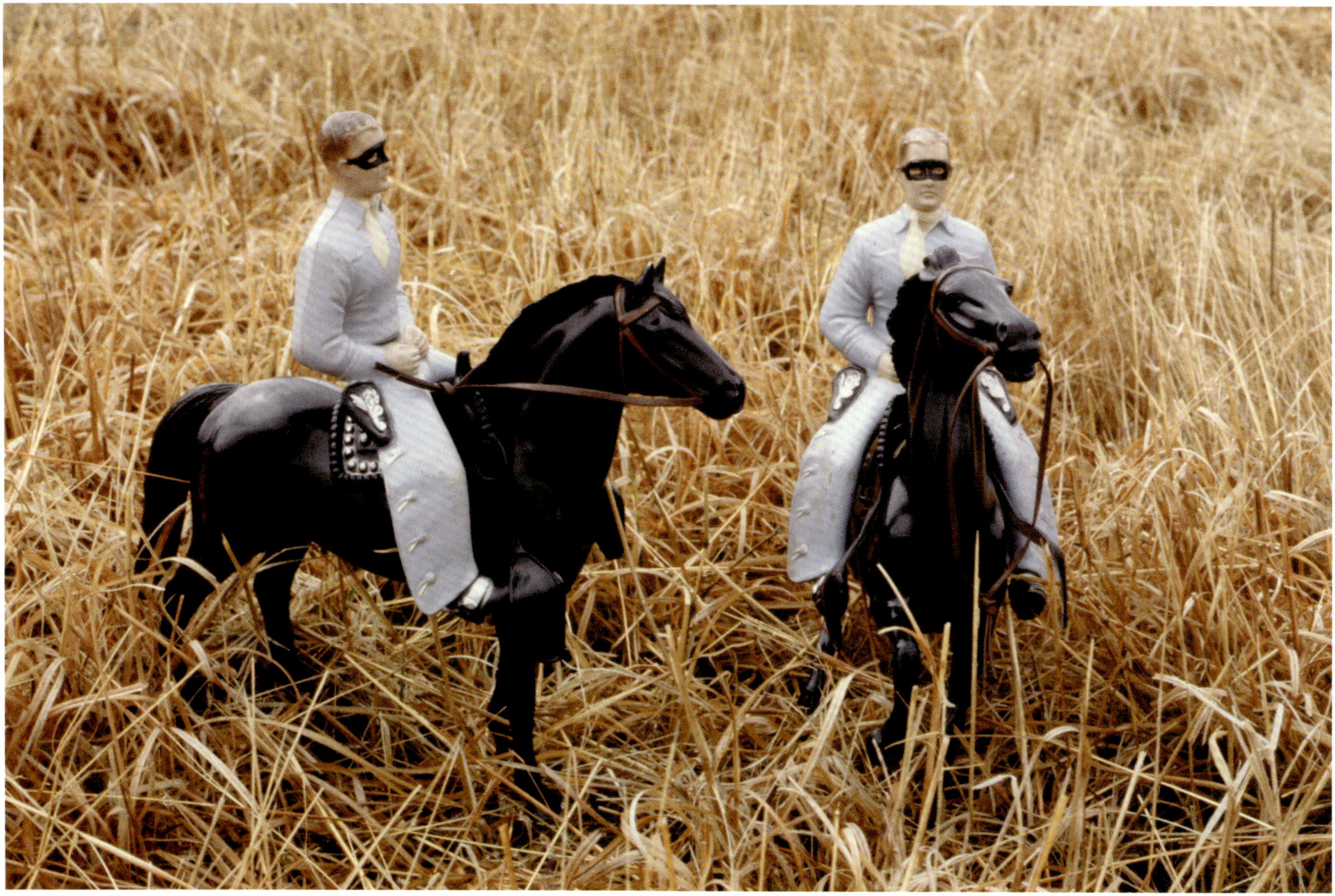

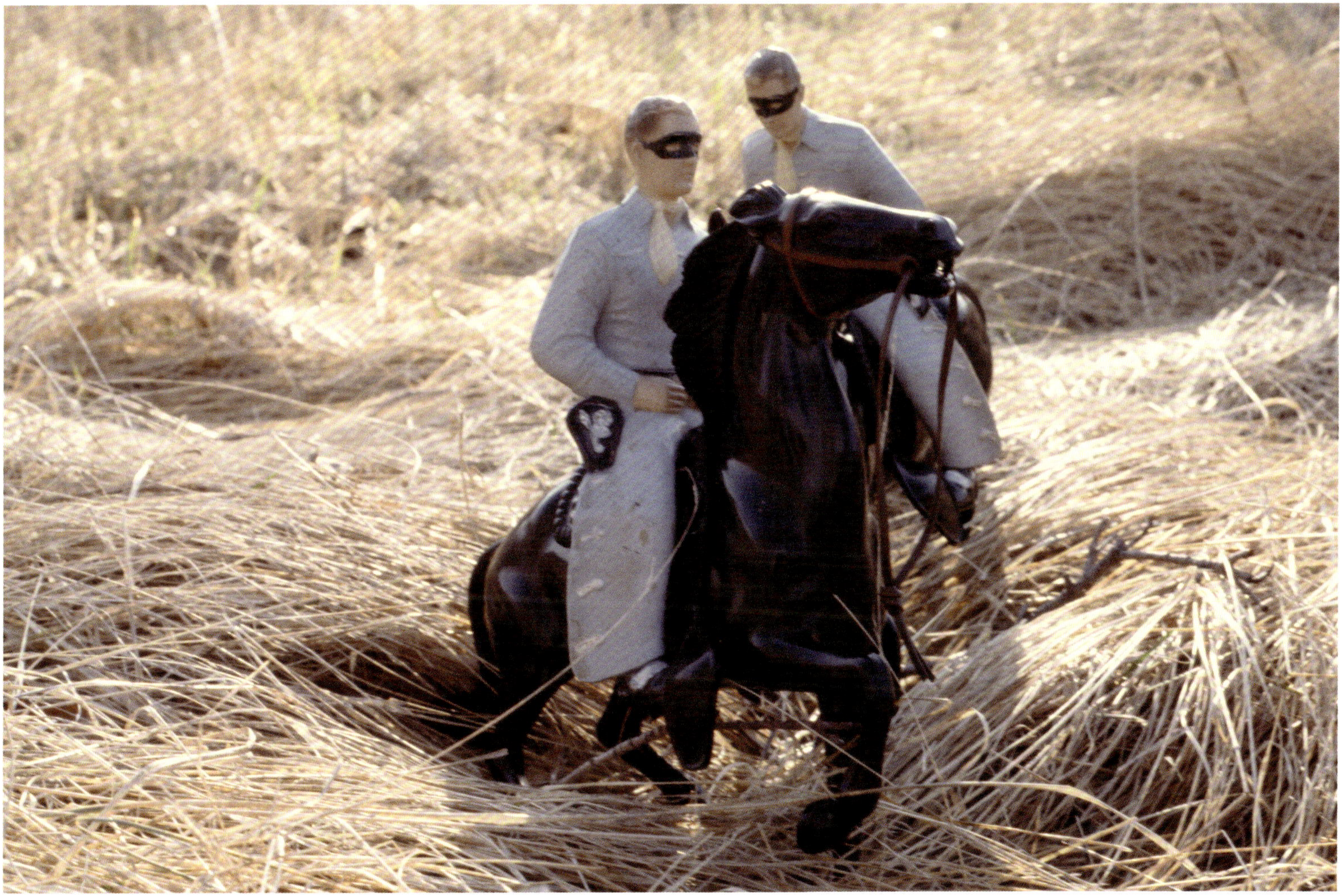

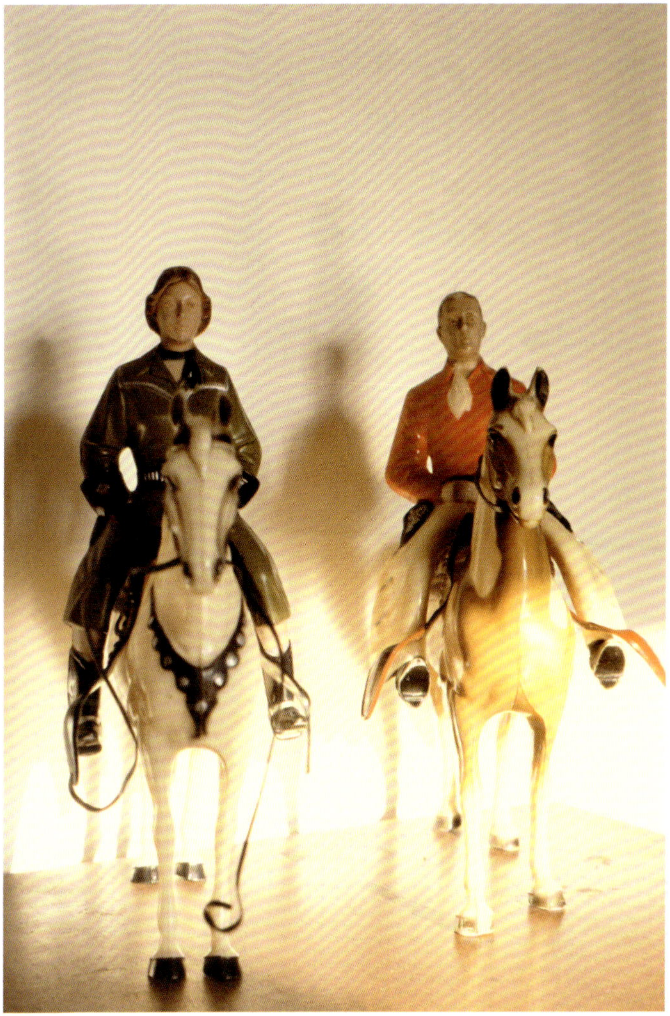

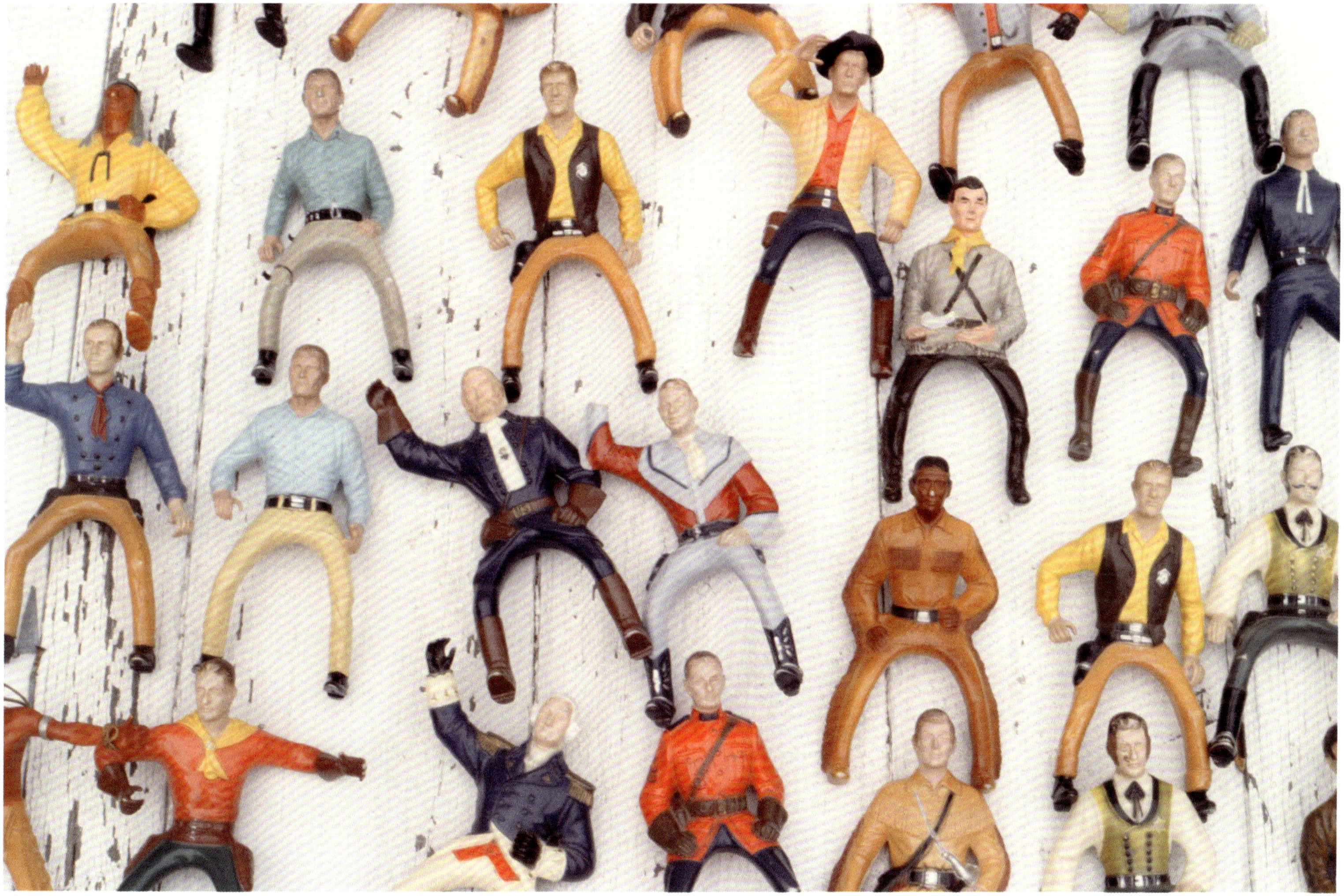

PAGE NUMBER	7	8	9
image credits	Blonde/Red Dress/Kitchen/Milk 1978 Cibachrome 3 1/2 x 5 inches Edition of 7 35 x 52 inches Edition of 3	New Kitchen/Aerial View 1979 Cibachrome 3 1/2 x 5 inches Edition of 7 35 x 52 inches Edition of 3	Woman Opening Refrigerator/Milk in the Middle 1979 Cibachrome print 3 1/2 x 5 inches Edition of 7 35 x 52 inches Edition of 3

10

New Kitchen/Aerial View/Seated
1979 Cibachrome

3 1/2 x 5 inches
Edition of 7

35 x 52 inches
Edition of 3

11

Blonde/Red Dress/Kitchen
1978 Cibachrome

3 1/2 x 5 inches
Edition of 7

35 x 52 inches
Edition of 3

12

Woman/Red Couch/Newspaper
1978 Cibachrome

3 1/2 x 5 inches
Edition of 7

35 x 52 inches
Edition of 3

14

Rabbit Shape
1978 Cibachrome

3 1/2 x 5 inches
Edition of 7

35 x 52 inches
Edition of 3

15

Light Room
1979 Cibachrome

6 x 9.5 inches
Edition of 7

35 x 52 inches
Edition of 3

16

Purple Woman/Gray Chair/Green Rug
1978 Cibachrome

3 1/2 x 5 inches
Edition of 7

35 x 52 inches
Edition of 3

17

Purple Woman/Gray Chair/Green Rug/Painting
1978 Cibachrome

3 1/2 x 5 inches
Edition of 7

35 x 52 inches
Edition of 3

18

Woman Reading Newspaper
1978 Cibachrome

3 1/2 x 5 inches
Edition of 7

35 x 52 inches
Edition of 3

19

Woman Watching TV
1978 Cibachrome

3 1/2 x 5 inches
Edition of 7

35 x 52 inches
Edition of 3

20

Purple Woman/Kitchen/Corner
1979 Cibachrome

3 1/2 x 5 inches
Edition of 7

35 x 52 inches
Edition of 3

21

Purple Woman/Kitchen
1978 Cibachrome

3 1/2 x 5 inches
Edition of 7

35 x 52 inches
Edition of 3

22

Purple Woman/Kitchen/Second View
1978 Cibachrome

3 1/2 x 5 inches
Edition of 7

35 x 52 inches
Edition of 3

25

Pushing Lipstick (Purple Woman)
1979 Cibachrome

5 3/4 x 8 3/4 inches
Edition of 7

35 x 52 inches
Edition of 3

27

Pushing Lipstick (Full Shadow)
1979 Cibachrome

5 3/4 x 8 3/4 inches
Edition of 7

35 x 52 inches
Edition of 3

28

Pushing Lipstick (Full Profile)
1979 Cibachrome

5 3/4 x 8 3/4 inches
Edition of 7

35 x 52 inches
Edition of 3

29

Pushing Lipstick (Red Lipstick)
1979 Cibachrome

5 3/4 x 8 3/4 inches
Edition of 7

35 x 52 inches
Edition of 3

30

Pushing Lipstick (Red Lipstick Vertical)
1979 Cibachrome

8 3/4 x 5 3/4 inches
Edition of 7

52 x 35 inches
Edition of 3

31

Pushing Lipstick (The Approach)
1979 Cibachrome

5 3/4 x 8 3/4 inches
Edition of 7

35 x 52 inches
Edition of 3

32

Pushing Lipstick (Spotlight)
1979 Cibachrome

5 3/4 x 8 3/4 inches
Edition of 7

35 x 52 inches
Edition of 3

35

First Bathroom/Woman Standing Left
1978 Cibachrome

3 1/2 x 5 inches
Edition of 7

35 x 52 inches
Edition of 3

36

First Bathroom/Woman Standing
1978 Cibachrome

3 1/2 x 5 inches
Edition of 7

35 x 52 inches
Edition of 3

37

New Bathroom/ Woman Standing
1979 Cibachrome

3 1/2 x 5 inches
Edition of 7

35 x 52 inches
Edition of 3

38

New Bathroom/Woman Standing/Sunlight
1979 Cibachrome

3 1/2 x 5 inches
Edition of 7

35 x 52 inches
Edition of 3

39

New Bathroom/Woman Kneeling/Second View
1979 Cibachrome

3 1/2 x 5 inches
Edition of 7

35 x 52 inches
Edition of 3

40

New Bathroom/Woman Kneeling/First View
1979 Cibachrome

3 1/2 x 5 inches
Edition of 7

35 x 52 inches
Edition of 3

41

First Bathroom/Woman Kneeling
1978 Cibachrome

3 1/2 x 5 inches
Edition of 7

35 x 52 inches
Edition of 3

42

New Bathroom/Aerial View/Sunlight
1979 Cibachrome

3 1/2 x 5 inches
Edition of 7

35 x 52 inches
Edition of 3

43

First Bathroom/Woman Standing/Vertical
1978 Cibachrome

5 x 3 1/2 inches
Edition of 7

52 x 35 inches
Edition of 3

44

New Bathroom Plan
1979 Cibachrome

3 1/2 x 5 inches
Edition of 7

35 x 52 inches
Edition of 3

47

Woman/Green Shirt/Red Barn
1979 Cibachrome

5 x 7 1/4 inches
Edition of 7

16 x 20 inches
Edition of 3

8 page text interlude by Collier Schorr

57

Man/Puddle
1979 Cibachrome

5 x 7 1/4 inches
Edition of 7

16 x 20 inches
Edition of 3

58

Horses/Slant
1979 Cibachrome

5 x 7 1/4 inches
Edition of 7

16 x 20 inches
Edition of 3

59

Man/Blue Shirt/Red Barn
1979 Cibachrome

5 x 7 1/4 inches
Edition of 7

16 x 20 inches
Edition of 3

60

Vertical/Man/Woman/Horse
1979 Cibachrome

7 1/4 x 5 inches
Edition of 7

20 x 16 inches
Edition of 3

61

Horizontal/Man/Woman/Horse
1979 Cibachrome

5 x 7 1/4 inches
Edition of 7

16 x 20 inches
Edition of 3

62

Man/Sky/Puddle/Second View
1979 Cibachrome

5 x 7 1/4 inches
Edition of 7

16 x 20 inches
Edition of 3

63

Man/Woman/Horse/Water
1979 Cibachrome

5 x 7 1/4 inches
Edition of 7

16 x 20 inches
Edition of 3

65

Brothers/Horizon
1979 Cibachrome

5 x 7 1/4 inches
Edition of 7

16 x 20 inches
Edition of 3

66

Brother/Aerial View/Vertical
1979 Cibachrome

7 1/4 x 5 inches
Edition of 7

20 x 16 inches
Edition of 3

67

Brothers/Aerial View
1979 Cibachrome

5 x 7 1/4 inches
Edition of 7

16 x 20 inches
Edition of 3

68

Brothers/No Horizon
1979 Cibachrome

5 x 7 1/4 inches
Edition of 7

16 x 20 inches
Edition of 3

69

Brothers/Hay
1979 Cibachrome

5 x 7 1/4 inches
Edition of 7

16 x 20 inches
Edition of 3

71

Woman/Man/Two Horses
1979 Cibachrome

7 1/4 x 5 inches
Edition of 7

20 x 16 inches
Edition of 3

73

Cowboy Pattern
1979 Cibachrome

5 x 7 1/4 inches
Edition of 7

16 x 20 inches
Edition of 3

Credits

Published on the occasion of the exhibition:

LAURIE SIMMONS
Photographs 1978/79

May 4 – June 29, 2002

Skarstedt Fine Art
1018 Madison Avenue New York, NY 10021
212-737 2060 tel 212-737 4171 fax
info@skarstedt.com

ISBN 0-9709090-3-9

The typefaces used in this book are Clarendon and ROSEWOOD FILL

Project Coordinators: Manuela Mozo and Leslie Fritz
Designed by: Honest, NYC
Printed in Iceland by Oddi Printers